Communism in ★
North Vietnam

Communism in
North Vietnam

ITS ROLE IN THE SINO-SOVIET DISPUTE

[P. J. HONEY]

THE M.I.T. PRESS, MASSACHUSETTS INSTITUTE OF TECHNOLOGY

CAMBRIDGE, MASSACHUSETTS

FOREWORD

This book is the second in a series that the Center for International Studies plans to publish in connection with its recently inaugurated project on international communism. The studies planned and in progress will continue the examination of the interaction between domestic factors in various countries affecting the local Communist parties and the impact from outside reflecting the growing disunity in the international Communist movement as a result of the Sino-Soviet rift and other developments. Geographically the project will be focused on three major areas: Europe, East and Southeast Asia, and Latin America, as well as on the Sino-Soviet rift itself.

Few countries and Communist parties are both less known and more important to American and Western foreign policy than North Vietnam. This book presents the first systematic, exhaustive analysis, based upon untranslated Vietnamese sources, of the tortuous course of

Hanoi's relations with Moscow and Peking. Mr. Honey, who is Lecturer in Vietnamese at the School of Oriental and African Studies of the University of London, is one of the West's leading authorities on Vietnam and the author of numerous studies on its politics.

Cambridge, Massachusetts
October 1963
WILLIAM E. GRIFFITH
Director, International Communism Project
Center for International Studies
Massachusetts Institute of Technology

PREFACE

Of the many inconsistencies to be found in the doctrines and beliefs of communism, the one which must strike the impartial observer most at the present time is the assumption that old-style internationalism is immune from the evolution which affects all political ideas. There is no little irony in the fact that China, the foremost advocate of world Communist unity, the one country committed by historical tradition to universalism, has been the force to wreck it. But the truth of the matter is that the stark pressures of national and international life in the mid-twentieth century have made such concepts as traditional internationalism, the abolition of national frontiers, and a monolithic Communist world appear utopian and impractical. In all parts of the world Communist parties are being obliged to identify themselves with national interests, and the form of communism which they practice is dictated as much by local national requirements as by Marxism-Leninism.

Any doubts about the truth of this assertion have already been dispelled by the antagonisms that exist between the Soviet Union and China. The withdrawal of Soviet technicians from China, the closing of Soviet consulates in China, the reduction of Soviet trade with China — the list of such incidents could be prolonged almost indefinitely — are recognizable symptoms of the great rift dividing Communists in all parts of the world, in both Communist and non-Communist countries. For the sake of brevity, students of Communist affairs tend to describe Communist countries or parties as pro-Soviet or pro-Chinese, but the divisions are more complex than this would suggest. They exist within national Communist parties and exercise a greater or lesser influence upon the conduct of these parties.

Following the Chinese armed attack against India in October 1962 numbers of Indian Communists appeared openly in the streets of Indian towns and cities to contribute to funds for the provision of comforts for Indian troops fighting against the Chinese People's Army. Indeed, in some cases, the Indian Communists organized such collections themselves. (BBC television program, "Panorama," Oct. 22, 1962, showed film of this.) Other sections of the Indian Communist Party, the pro-Chinese wing, took no part in this activity and remained off the streets, fearing the dangers of public support for China in the prevailing atmosphere of bitter Indian resentment against Chinese actions.

In the course of the dispute between the Soviet Union and China the issues at stake have become reasonably well defined. The positions adopted by most of the countries in the Communist bloc too have become apparent so that it is possible to forecast with a high degree of accuracy which Communist giant each will support when a new clash of interests looms over the horizon. Only in one or two cases is there any doubt, and the reasons for the nonaligned situation of these countries are to be found in local conditions.

Of all the countries under Communist rule at the present time Communist North Vietnam presents the greatest enigma insofar as her position in the Sino-Soviet dispute is concerned. Unlike other Communist states, she did not commit herself wholly to the side of the Soviet Union or China but has steered a somewhat erratic middle course, veering sometimes closer to the one and sometimes to the other. Perfectly valid reasons have dictated each move of the Vietnamese Communist regime since the outbreak of the Sino-Soviet dispute, but these can be fully understood only when the special factors peculiar to North Vietnam and the sequence of events leading up to the formation of a Communist state in North Vietnam are familiar. For that reason, the first part of this study is devoted to a brief examination of the more important factors influencing the behavior of North Vietnam in the context of the Sino-Soviet dispute.

P. J. Honey

University of London
July 1963

CONTENTS

LIST OF ABBREVIATIONS

CCP   Chinese Communist Party

CMEA   Council for Mutual Economic Assistance

CPR   Chinese People's Republic

CPSU   Communist Party of the Soviet Union

DRV   Democratic Republic of Vietnam (Communist North Vietnam)

ICC   International Control Commission

NCNA   New China News Agency

NFLSV National Front for the Liberation of South Vietnam

PRP   People's Revolutionary Party (South Vietnam)

VNA   Vietnam News Agency (North Vietnam)

WFTU   World Federation of Trade Unions

FACTORS BEARING ON
NORTH VIETNAMESE POLICIES

GEOGRAPHICAL SITUATION

North Vietnam lies to the south of China, with whom she shares a long frontier. This geographical situation of their country has engendered in the North Vietnamese people an attitude of mind toward China not dissimilar from that of the Sicilians who live on the slopes of Mount Etna toward the volcano. Both have been obliged by the circumstances of geography to live in the close proximity of a mighty force which, although it lies dormant for very long periods, is capable of violent, uncontrollable eruption at any time and with very little warning. In such a situation people develop a constant sense of awareness, a sensitivity to signs likely to presage violent movement, which influences the whole of their lives and actions. The awareness of this latent danger to the independence of their country has been present among the Vietnamese for some thousands of years and is as alive today as it ever was in the past.

Twice in the course of her recorded history Vietnam has been annexed by China, being obliged to undergo Chinese domination for a thousand years on the first occasion but only twenty years on the second. Several Chinese attacks against Vietnam have been repulsed by armed force, and even the vast Mongol armies of Kublai Khan were defeated by the Vietnamese and forced back into China. But armed clashes against Chinese invaders have always proved costly enterprises involving heavy damage to property, great loss of life, and serious hardships and suffering among the population. The Vietnamese have for the most part preferred to employ a more subtle policy of political dissuasion to prevent Chinese irruptions into their land.

The essence of successful politics is intelligent compromise, and for many centuries the Vietnamese made concessions to their powerful northern neighbor and thereby contrived to preserve their independence. They acknowledged China as a suzerain state and permitted the Chinese court to perform the ceremony of investiture for Vietnamese emperors, and at regular intervals the Vietnamese sent tribute to the Emperor of China; but the cost of such concessions was small. In return they maintained the right to govern Vietnam without Chinese interference, to administer the country in any way they thought fit, and to select their own emperors even if the Chinese performed the coronation ceremony. In brief, the Vietnamese were content to pay lip service to Chinese pretensions provided they themselves retained the reins of power in Vietnam.

With the establishment of French control over Indochina during the latter part of the nineteenth century the necessity for the Vietnamese rulers to safeguard their country against China disappeared. The task fell to France and did not prove difficult because the period of French domination coincided with an age of Chinese weakness. Not until the middle of the twentieth century was China united under a strong central government, and it was Chinese aid to the Vietnamese Communist resistance which more than any other single factor ended French rule in Vietnam. When the Geneva Conference of 1954 accorded independence to Vietnam, the perennial problem of how to deal with China was again placed upon Vietnamese shoulders, and in spite of the shared political creed of communism the North Vietnamese entertained few illusions about the nature of the Chinese. They were keenly aware, and especially their Communist leaders, of the renewed national danger.

THE VIETNAMESE AND THE CHINESE

The attitude of virtually all Vietnamese toward the Chinese is complex and difficult to describe. There is certainly a very strong element of dislike in it, stemming from past Chinese injustices. Stories of the greed, the duplicity, and the terrible cruelty of the Chinese rulers during the two periods of Chinese domination abound in Vietnam and are recounted as though the events of history had taken place only recently. Vietnamese feelings toward the Chinese are not unlike those of the Irish for the English of Oliver Cromwell's day. When Chinese troops occupied North Vietnam for a few months after World War II, their behavior justified all Vietnamese fears, for they pillaged, stole, cheated, and took with them from the country everything of value that was movable.

Mixed with dislike is an understandable apprehension that springs not only from the great size and the expansionist tendencies of China but also from the Chinese capacity for trade and commerce, in which they repeatedly outstrip the Vietnamese. Under French rule in Indochina a very large portion of Vietnam's wealth was in the hands of a Chinese minority that monopolized lucrative sections of the country's business.

Yet in spite of all, there remains a feeling of kinship with the Chinese and a genuine respect for Chinese cultural achievements. The Vietnamese feels more at home with the Chinese than with any other foreigners. Possibly this is owing to the racial affinities of the two peoples and to the traditions and institutions of a common civilization. Certainly the Vietnamese are among the most color-conscious people in the world, and the Chinese are ethnically similar enough to them to avoid causing distaste on this score.

Nevertheless, the overriding emotion of the Vietnamese is dislike, and that is why Communist campaigns stressing the "historical friendship" between the peoples of Vietnam and China had to be abandoned hurriedly when they encountered so much ridicule in North Vietnam. It is interesting to note that many of the new factories and industrial undertakings in North Vietnam have been named after Vietnamese heroes venerated because of their victories over Chinese invaders, and that the anniversary of the Emperor Quang Trung, who not only defeated a Chinese army but also laid claim to territory in southern China during the eighteenth century, is celebrated annually by the Communist authorities.

In the present circumstances it would seem reasonable to expect the Communist leaders of North Vietnam to revert to the earlier Vietnamese policy of paying lip service to China, of making concessions to China provided these did not permit the Chinese actively to participate in the government of Vietnam, and of guarding jealously their own right to run the country without interference from outside. Events may well prove that such a policy can no longer be followed today, that the Chinese will demand to play an important part in Vietnamese affairs; but until that time comes, this is the policy that will probably be uppermost in the minds of the Vietnamese leaders.

PRESSURES FOR REUNIFICATION

The Geneva agreements of 1954, which ended the long Indochinese war, gave far less to the Vietnamese Communists than even their most pessimistic supporters could have expected. After a struggle in which they had unquestionably defeated their opponents, and despite the great military victory of Dienbienphu, the Communists were granted control over only the northern half of Vietnam and were obliged to accept the presence of an International Control Commission on their territory. In signing the agreements they were forced to bow to strong Soviet pressure, a fact that robbed them of much prestige at home, and the only face-saving concession made to them was the unsigned "Declaration of Intention," which prescribed national elections for the reunification of Vietnam, to be held not later than July 1956. The worthlessness of this concession can be seen in a remark made by the Communist North Vietnam (DRV)[1] Prime Minister, Pham Van Dong, to one of my Vietnamese friends immediately after the signing of the agreements. When asked which side he thought would win the elections, Dong replied, "You know as well as I do that there won't be any elections."

DRV policy following the Geneva agreements was to consolidate the Communist position in North Vietnam while waiting for the South to collapse under the weight of its own serious internal dissensions. But, contrary to all expectations, Ngo Dinh Diem overcame the difficulties besetting his government, and it was South Vietnam, not North Vietnam, which began to make rapid progress. North Vietnam sustained grave setbacks, the most important of which was the failure of its agrarian reform campaign. South Vietnam's success was due in very large measure to the massive aid that she received from the United States, a fact that led North Vietnam to regard the United States as her principal enemy and the most serious threat to her security.

As no national elections were held in Vietnam during 1956, the "Declaration of Intention" became a dead letter, and the two halves of the country remained divided. In consequence, the Vietnamese Communists lost their earlier reputation for invincibility and found that they had to contend with the continuing existence of a rival Vietnamese government which constituted an ever-present threat to the authority of their regime in

[1] Since Communist North Vietnam calls itself the Democratic Republic of Vietnam, it is commonly referred to by the initials DRV; for the sake of brevity that usage is employed hereafter in the text.

North Vietnam. They employed subversion inside South Vietnam in an attempt to overthrow the government of President Ngo Dinh Diem and to replace it with another less likely to resist Communist pressures, but their efforts met with little success. Once again it was American support and aid that enabled President Diem to resist Communist attempts to undermine his regime. During the latter half of 1959 the Communists changed their tactics in the South and resorted to sabotage, murder, and armed insurrection. As more and more Communist guerrillas were infiltrated from the North, the scale and extent of armed resistance increased and the threat to President Diem's government became greater. Again the United States came to the assistance of South Vietnam with military instructors and equipment, later adding airplanes and helicopters flown by American pilots. The struggle still continues, and each new Communist effort is matched with such United States aid as is necessary to check and overcome it.

Thus the Communist leadership of North Vietnam has lost a great measure of its earlier ascendancy because of the failure to reunify the country, is faced by a rival government in South Vietnam which has defied Communist efforts to overthrow it since 1954, and in its struggle to annex South Vietnam finds itself thwarted by United States aid to President Diem. For these reasons its situation bears a close resemblance to that of the Chinese Communist leadership which has been unable to annex Formosa and dispose of the rival Chinese government of Chiang Kai-shek because of American support for the latter. Communist China can therefore feel assured of a genuine sympathy among Vietnamese Communists for its bitter antipathy toward the United States, for its impatience with the Soviet interpretation of peaceful coexistence, and for its belligerent attitude. The links forged between North Vietnam and China by the similarity of both countries' circumstances do exert a perceptible influence upon the formation of Vietnamese attitudes toward China and the Soviet Union.

THE ECONOMIC SITUATION

North Vietnam is largely mountainous, and almost all its Vietnamese population is concentrated in the overcrowded delta of the Red River. By tradition the Vietnamese are a people of the plains, on which they produce their staple food, rice. In the past they have shunned the upland regions, leaving them to the minority peoples, the Meos, the Thos, the Nungs, the Lolos, and others. As a result the lowlands of North Vietnam are grossly overpopulated while the highlands are very sparsely inhabited. Throughout the period of French control in Indochina North Vietnam was not self-supporting in food, but its deficit was easily offset by the transfer of surplus rice from the South to the North. Today, however, the two halves of Vietnam are divided, and no traffic passes across the line of the seventeenth parallel, which separates North from South. Since the division of Vietnam in 1954 the DRV authorities have been unable to obtain rice freely from South Vietnam and have had to contend with chronic food shortages. Although they have greatly increased the area under cultivation and have endeavored to supplement rice with secondary crops such as maize and sweet potatoes, agricultural production has been held back by the enforced collectivization of land which has antagonized peasants and reduced productivity. A fear never absent from the minds of the Vietnamese Communist leaders is that of national famine, a disaster capable of toppling their regime in North Vietnam.

The situation was well known to the DRV leaders when the Geneva agreements were signed in 1954, but they were obliged by the Soviet Union to accept those agreements. At the time they were not too greatly worried by the problem because they were convinced that strife-ridden South Vietnam could not long continue to enjoy a separate existence but would quickly fall victim to their own greater military strength and political experience. Had there been no United States aid forthcoming, the probability is that their expectations would have been fulfilled, but events moved differently, and South Vietnam soon began to show signs of resisting Communist efforts indefinitely. The DRV leaders found themselves face to face with a serious and recurring food shortage.

In common with all Communist states, North Vietnam adheres to the belief that the true basis of power is the proletariat. It was embarrassed by the fact that it possessed none in 1954, or rather that its proletariat was so small that it would have been ridiculous to think of basing anything upon it. Like China she was greatly concerned with creating a body of industrial workers in the shortest possible time. In the meanwhile she subscribed to Mao Tse-tung's pronouncements such as "advancing on two legs," which defined the contribution of the peasantry. Both the economic situation of North Vietnam and the likelihood that South Vietnam would remain independent for a long time combined with the need for a worker proletariat to dictate the country's economic planning.

Reduced to the simplest terms, North Vietnam's economic policy set the following goals:

1. To expand agriculture as rapidly and as widely as possible so as to produce at home as much of the country's food needs as conditions would permit.

2. To create a modern industry in the shortest possible time so as to be able to earn foreign currency from the sale of manufactured goods abroad. This money could then be used to purchase enough food to make good the foreign trade deficit.

3. To exploit the mineral deposits reputed to exist in the uplands. These would be used to supply raw materials for the factories and for further exports.

Parts 2 and 3 of the plan when fully carried out would supply the longed-for proletariat and fulfill the country's economic needs.

These goals are of course an oversimplification of DRV economic planning, but they do convey the broad outlines of policy. Many mistakes have been made in their execution and lessons have been learned from repeated failures, but some progress has been made in industrialization. Contrary to the belief that was widespread among Vietnamese Communists, the process of industrialization requires a long time; peasants cannot be turned into industrial workers overnight. At the time of this writing some factories have been completed and more are under construction. Vietnamese are gradually acquiring industrial skills, and the small proletariat has been expanded, though it is still very far from large. The quality of the manufactured products is pitifully low, and many of them have had to be scrapped because they proved to be unusable.[2]

Early in the process of industrialization the DRV leaders became acutely aware of a fact that was to exert a very important influence upon their future actions in the dispute between the Soviet Union and China: Only the Soviet Union and the European satellites could supply the modern machines needed to equip the new factories. In the early days of independence, when the emphasis was upon repairing war damage, replacing bridges, re-laying torn-up railway track, and restoring roads to a usable condition, Chinese assistance was found to be very valuable. China sent low-grade technicians capable of directing Vietnamese labor in the carrying out of these tasks, and the Vietnamese Communists were grateful. But when the moment arrived for the industrialization program to get under way, it became apparent to all that China lacked both the technicians and the equipment. If North Vietnam were to build an industry, it would have to depend almost entirely upon help supplied by the Soviet Union and her European satellites. For this reason, if for no other, it was necessary for North Vietnam to remain on good terms with the Soviet Union.

EXPERIENCE WITH CHINESE-STYLE COMMUNISM

Following the victory of Mao Tse-tung in 1949 the Vietnamese resistance movement began to receive military and other aid from China. Without it the Viet-

[2] For fuller details, see *China News Analysis*, No. 460, Mar. 15, 1963.

namese Communists might never have brought their long drawn-out struggle to a successful conclusion, but the acceptance of such aid meant that a large measure of political direction would also have to be accepted. Undoubtedly there were many, probably even a majority, among the Vietnamese Communists who felt that Mao Tse-tung's doctrinal innovations were more directly applicable to Vietnamese conditions than the unmodified teachings of Marx, Engels, Lenin, and Stalin. Mao was, after all, speaking about a situation which was not dissimilar from that in Vietnam, and it is not surprising to find that North Vietnam followed Chinese actions and policies very closely in the early years.

The first shock of disillusionment with Chinese policies came with the disastrous failure of the agrarian reform in North Vietnam. In carrying out the reform the Vietnamese Communists slavishly followed the Chinese model, and each of the agrarian reform teams of cadres was advised and supervised by Chinese instructors. The Vietnamese cadres themselves were obliged to spend long periods studying Chinese experiences in this field before they commenced work.[3] Truong Chinh, then Secretary-General of the Lao Dong Party[4] and perhaps

[3] See Hoang Van Chi, *From Colonialism to Communism* (New York: Frederick A. Praeger, 1963).

[4] In 1929 there were three rival Communist parties in Vietnam. In January 1930 Ho Chi Minh conferred with delegates from these different parties in Hong Kong and persuaded them to amalgamate so as to form a single party, the Vietnamese Communist Party. At a Communist congress held in Hong Kong during October of the same year, the name was changed to the Indochinese Communist Party. This party was formally dissolved in November 1945 because it was proving an impediment to the formation of a national united front to combat the French authorities in Indochina, though it is interesting to note that an Association for Marxist Studies was formed on the very day of its dissolution. That the dissolution was no more than a tactical move was shown by the Cominform journal of Aug. 21,

the greatest admirer of Chinese communism in the whole of the DRV leadership, publicly associated himself with the reform and even went so far as to refer to the special cadres appointed to carry it out as "my cadres" on several occasions. Far from proving the success he had forecast, the agrarian reform incensed the people of North Vietnam more than any other Communist action before or since. Revolts flared up locally and had to be forcibly suppressed, and public anger rose to such heights as to threaten the very existence of the Lao Dong Party. Never before had the Vietnamese Communists made such a mistake, and Ho Chi Minh himself was obliged to assume the post of Party Secretary-General, ordering Truong Chinh to resign and to make a public self-criticism so as to ensure the continuation of the Communist regime. Yet the real blame belonged to the Chinese, who had directed the Vietnamese at every stage of the reform. The myth of Mao's infallibility was already exploded for the Vietnamese.

The decision to abandon the slavish imitation of China appears to have come with the failure in Vietnam

---

1953, which recorded that the Communist Party membership in Vietnam had increased from 20,000 in 1946 to 500,000 in 1950, a period during which there was — officially at least — no Communist Party in Vietnam. The Communist Party made its official reappearance in early 1951, when it assumed the new name Dang Lao Dong Viet Nam, or Vietnamese Workers' Party. The reason for the choice of the new name was, according to a party document captured by the French, to remove a source of resentment against the Vietnamese felt by members of the Cambodian and Laotian resistance movements. It was felt that three national Communist parties should be formed to replace the old Indochinese Communist Party so that Laotians and Cambodians fighting against the French might not feel that Vietnamese Communists were directing their own national resistance movements. Needless to say, the Vietnamese continued to direct these movements, but they acted through the medium of Cambodian Communists. In this study the Vietnamese Communist Party is referred to throughout as the Lao Dong Party.

of Mao's "Hundred Flowers" campaign. The North Vietnamese people were profoundly affected by the attacks on their regime published in the new newspapers which first appeared at the beginning of the campaign, and once again the Communist regime was seriously threatened. Ho Chi Minh felt constrained to intervene so hurriedly that he shut down the offending newspapers even before he was able to produce the "spontaneous" petitions from the people demanding their closure. While it lasted, the "Hundred Flowers" campaign seriously undermined the authority of the Communist leaders inside Vietnam and exposed to the outside world the true situation that had hitherto remained concealed behind a formidable barrage of propaganda lies.[5]

The end of the North Vietnamese–Chinese honeymoon dates from 1957, and it is interesting to note that Ho Chi Minh made no attempt to imitate such Chinese policies as the "Great Leap Forward" and the creation of communes. Their own experiences with some Chinese policies and their knowledge of the failure of some others not copied in Vietnam must have engendered in every Vietnamese Communist a healthy skepticism about the wisdom of any policy put forward by the Chinese. Certainly these things must affect Vietnamese attitudes and actions in the Sino-Soviet dispute.

THE EFFECTS OF DIVISION

As in most Communist states, the vast majority of the people in North Vietnam have not supported the doctrine of communism and still do not approve of it.

[5] See P. J. Honey, "Revolt of the Intellectuals in North Vietnam," *The World Today*, XIII, 6 (June 1957).

The Communist regime was imposed on North Vietnam by Ho Chi Minh's clever exploitation of Vietnamese nationalism, which was nationwide, for his own Communist ends. He was enabled to do this because the nationalist resistance movement had to rely upon China and the other countries of the Communist bloc for arms, supplies, and training. By directing supplies to the Vietnamese Communists, the Chinese obliged the nationalists to depend upon these men, with the result that the Communists acquired a dominance over the whole resistance movement which was out of all proportion to their small numbers and which permitted them to seize and maintain control of the movement. In this way the Communists, although numerically only a tiny minority in 1945, had contrived to assume unchallenged leadership of the resistance by the end of the Indochinese war in 1954 and were able to establish their regime in North Vietnam.

The fiction that the Vietnamese resistance movement was basically a nationalist movement in which some Communists played a part, not a movement dominated and tightly controlled by Communists, was continued until the end of the war. It had to be, for the success of the resistance depended in very large measure upon the help it received from Vietnamese civilians living within the French-held zones. These provided money, food, medicines, intelligence of enemy movements, and much else besides. It is highly improbable that assistance on such a scale would have been given to a self-confessed Communist-led movement struggling to establish a Communist regime; consequently, Ho Chi Minh found it necessary to create the elaborate front organization, the Lien Viet, of which the Lao Dong Party was only one

of several member bodies. To sustain the fiction he appointed a number of Vietnamese known to be non-Communists to some of the highest offices in the government. It scarcely needs to be said that, although they enjoyed the titles and outward trappings of these high posts, the power rested in the hands of a trustworthy party member who acted as assistant, or adviser, or held some other such less exalted office.

After the end of the war, when Vietnam was split into two zones, Ho Chi Minh found that it was still necessary to beguile the people of South Vietnam who were not, and are not today, pro-Communist. It was no longer possible to conceal the Communist nature of the DRV regime, but he was still able to reassure many of the non-Communists in the South by pointing to his non-Communist ministers and deputy ministers. The implication was that it is possible to rise to the highest positions in North Vietnam even if one is not a member of the Lao Dong Party. That is the reason why the democrat Phan Anh is the DRV Minister for Foreign Trade; another democrat, Tran Dang Khoa, is Minister for Irrigation; socialist Hoang Minh Giam is Minister of Culture, and so on. Yet the nonparty Minister of Education, Nguyen Van Huyen, confessed to a friend who subsequently fled to South Vietnam that all important decisions were taken by the Lao Dong Party and that he himself was never consulted.

Perhaps the most surprising appointment of all was that of Phan Ke Toai as the DRV Minister of the Interior and a Deputy Premier. Toai's mandarinal origins could scarcely have been more bourgeois, and in 1945 he was the Emperor Bao Dai's Imperial Delegate to North Vietnam. He surrendered his office to Ho Chi

Minh and was given a high post in Ho's administration
— primarily because his name was well known and would
lend an air of respectability to that illegal body. At first
glance it may appear curious that such a person could
occupy so important a ministry as the Interior, but the
functions normally associated with this ministry are in
North Vietnam carried out by two other organizations,
the Ministry of Public Security and the Department of
Internal Affairs in the Premier's Office. Both are directed
by the same man, Tran Quoc Hoan, an alternate member of the Lao Dong Party Politburo. (On April 30, 1963
the DRV National Assembly dismissed Phan Ke Toai
from his post of Minister of the Interior "at his own
request and for reasons of age." It also dismissed the
Communist Ung Van Khiem from his post of Foreign
Minister, giving no reasons for this, and appointed him
Minister of the Interior.)

A further consequence of partition is that the DRV
leadership is disinclined to adopt any measures or policies which might antagonize public opinion in South
Vietnam and make the task of reunification more
difficult. Whatever individual DRV leaders may have
thought privately about China's communes, no mention
was made of them in the press, on the radio, or in
public speeches. It was rightly calculated that they would
horrify South Vietnamese opinion and so could not be
copied in North Vietnam or even discussed publicly.
Thus the necessity to avoid offending the people of
South Vietnam, as distinct from the government, has
for long exercised a restraining influence upon the rulers
of North Vietnam and will continue to do so as long as
partition remains. Non-Communist ministers and officials will have to be retained in office, and their public

functions will have to be arranged so as not to disclose the fact that they are mere puppets, window dressing to secure the approbation of unwary South Vietnamese. The general tendency is for North Vietnam to avoid actions or statements that might be considered too extremist.

Moreover, antagonism of long standing exists between the peoples of North and South Vietnam. The halves were divided for roughly two hundred years between the end of the sixteenth and the end of the eighteenth centuries — the dividing line was remarkably close to the present one — and a state of war existed between them. To counteract the residual suspicion of the North that still persists in the South, the DRV regime has been obliged to promote South Vietnamese adherents to high positions in the government and the Lao Dong Party simply because they were born in South Vietnam and not because of their outstanding ability. Ung Van Khiem, for example, a man remarkable only for the gaffes he has committed — and survived unscathed — was DRV Foreign Minister as well as a member of the Lao Dong Party Central Committee, and there are others like him who have received unmerited promotion. Such men have to be accorded the full powers that their positions warrant lest they take offense and cause embarrassment. As a result they constitute a source of weakness in the leadership.

THE LEADERSHIP ★

2

To understand the actions of any government, the reasons for them and their implications, and to be able to forecast with a reasonable degree of accuracy the course likely to be followed by that government in the future, it is necessary to know not only the internal and international situation of the country that it governs but also the political inclinations of the individual members, the amount of power and influence each commands, and something of the historical background which led to the formation of the government. This may appear to state the obvious, but it is a fact that very few of those who study and comment on Communist North Vietnam have taken the trouble to acquire such information about its leadership, and as a result much that has been written about this Vietnamese Communist state is inaccurate and misleading. There is no space here for a thorough study of the DRV leadership, but some of the

essential facts must be set out, albeit briefly, in order
that its behavior may be understood.

One feature that has impressed outside observers is
its remarkable stability; it has remained in power with
only few major changes of personnel for many years.
This phenomenon has not come about accidentally but
is the result of the conscious and deliberate efforts of
one man. The source of all authority in North Vietnam
is and always has been the Head of State and Chairman
of the Lao Dong Party, Ho Chi Minh. Ho has deemed
it important to create the impression of a stable and
monolithic leadership, and to this end he has been
reluctant to make any changes in personnel except when
forced to. In consequence he has found it necessary to
retain in office men who exercise no political power or
influence and to insist that they receive all the public
marks of respect to which their high positions in the
state entitle them. This practice has necessitated much
administrative inconvenience, but Ho obviously believes
that its rewards outweigh its disadvantages.

Second in importance to Ho Chi Minh are the twelve
other members of the Politburo of the Lao Dong Party,
ten of whom are full members and the remaining two
alternate members. Not all of these men enjoy equal
influence. The two alternate members, who are responsible for state security, owe their membership to the
official posts that they occupy in the government; and
there is reason for believing that two of the full members
are protégés of other Politburo members and are less
powerful than their colleagues for that reason. Therefore
in effect there are eight people who form the second
echelon of the North Vietnamese leadership.[1]

[1] The full members of the Lao Dong Party Politburo are as follows:

Rivalries and enmities exist among the eight, and the group is monolithic in outward appearance only. Since the causes of personal differences are various, stemming from personal antipathies, political differences, conflicting ambitions, and so on, a skilled and experienced politician such as Ho Chi Minh does not find it too difficult to play one off against the other and thus maintain his own supremacy. The fact that he is now a very old man (by Vietnamese standards) who cannot hope to continue his leadership indefinitely can only serve to exacerbate mutual antagonisms within the Politburo, each of whose members must already be greatly exercised over the question of Ho's successor.

Below the Politburo stands the Central Committee of the Lao Dong Party, the list of whose membership was first published in September 1960. According to the official pronouncement this body comprises 71 members, of whom 43 are full members and 28 alternate members, but information has subsequently come to light which indicates that the published list of members was incomplete. The identity of additional Central Committee members and even their very existence were kept secret because these men are today directing the Vietcong insurgents in South Vietnam, and the DRV leadership has repeatedly claimed that North Vietnam has no

---

Ho Chi Minh, Chairman of the Lao Dong Party
Le Duan, First Secretary of the Lao Dong Party
Truong Chinh, former Secretary-General of the Lao Dong Party
Pham Van Dong
Vo Nguyen Giap
Le Duc Tho
Nguyen Duy Trinh
Nguyen Chi Thanh, believed to be a protégé of Truong Chinh
Pham Hung, believed to be a protégé of Pham Van Dong
Le Thanh Nghi
Hoang Van Hoan

connection with the war in the South.[2] It is therefore not possible to state the exact strength of the Central Committee, but the total membership is probably less than one hundred. Members of the body fill the key posts in the DRV government, army, parliament, and all other important institutions as well as in the Lao Dong Party machine. Ho Chi Minh, the Politburo, and the Central Committee make all important decisions in North Vietnam and supervise their execution. Although members of the Central Committee do not always occupy the highest offices in the organizations where they serve, it is they, not the nominal leaders, who control these bodies.

In addition there are large numbers of Lao Dong Party members of long standing whose loyalty and reliability have been proved beyond doubt. These persons occupy positions within all the organs of the state and are carefully deployed so as to be able to supervise the correct carrying out of party decisions and to report any instances of failure. Lao Dong Party members are not numerous enough to fill all the important administrative and executive positions in the state even if this were considered desirable, but much the same results are obtained by placing one or two inside every undertaking and granting them wide powers to direct or report upon their colleagues. Non-Communist Vietnamese

[2] After the international agreements on Laotian neutrality had been signed at Geneva in July 1962, a senior member of the DRV delegation inadvertently disclosed in the presence of foreign press correspondents that secret members of the Central Committee were directing Vietcong operations in South Vietnam. He named four such men — Pham Van Dang, Nguyen Van Cuc, Le Toan Thu, and Pham Thai Buong — and gave the impression there were others besides. The incident, which has since appeared in several publications, was first reported in a British newspaper, *The Sunday Telegraph,* on July 29, 1962.

occupy technical posts and even very high administrative or political posts but exert only an insignificant influence upon the determination of policy.

Viewed from the outside, North Vietnam presents the appearance of a state endowed with a stable and experienced government, Communist-led of course, and not overfond of holding elections, but one in which non-Communists occupy many top positions and seem to work amicably alongside their party colleagues. It is a carefully contrived public image and one which deceives the casual observer, but closer study reveals that the Lao Dong Party members, and only they, have an effective voice in national affairs. The non-Communist ministers, directors, and chiefs, for all their exalted designations, are powerless to do anything except carry out the directives of the party.

So long as Ho Chi Minh continues to hold the reins of power, North Vietnam will enjoy the benefits of his long experience in international politics and of his great political ability. He alone decides upon questions of high policy, while the rest, even the members of the Politburo, simply accept and implement his orders in these matters. For the moment his pre-eminent position is unchallenged. By exploiting the rivalries that divide the members of the Politburo he is able to secure obedience from all of them, and he derives other advantages from the different shades of political opinion which these men represent. When he wishes to change one current policy for another, he merely withdraws his support from the protagonist of that policy and transfers it to the man who best reflects the other. Dependent upon Ho for their political power and influence, the Politburo members have no choice but to concur in his decisions.

None can now afford to oppose him, especially since he is an old man and may be expected to play an important part in the selection of his eventual successor.

The second DRV constitution, which was adopted in 1960, made provision for the appointment of a Vice-President, and the Politburo must have awaited Ho's choice with some apprehension, for it was not unnatural to expect that the man appointed to the office could hope to succeed Ho. Ho Chi Minh selected Ton Duc Thang as Vice-President, a man with an exemplary revolutionary past but one who was even older than Ho himself and already showing signs of senility. Clearly Ho was unwilling to single out a potential successor and thereby risk the weakening of his own power.

HO CHI MINH

The political career of Ho Chi Minh extends backward in time as far as the First World War. A member of the now famous Congress of French Socialists at Tours in 1920, where the decision to form the French Communist Party was taken, Ho subsequently traveled to Moscow as a French delegate and remained there to study communism and its techniques. In 1925 he appeared in China, ostensibly to work at the Soviet Consulate in Canton but in reality to commence his career as an agent of international communism. Although his duties for the Comintern extended to a number of other Asian countries, it was Ho who laid the foundations of communism in Vietnam and, in 1930, was chiefly responsible for the creation of the Indochinese Communist Party. His Comintern duties did not permit him to remain in Vietnam and lead this party but required him to spend the greater part of his time abroad. It is worthy of note, and possibly significant for the future, that the fortunes of the Indochinese Communist Party prospered when the body was led by Ho himself but invariably slumped during his absences. The other leaders of Vietnamese communism, most of whom are to be found today in the Politburo or Central Committee of the Lao Dong Party, appeared to be incapable of directing the party by themselves. Perhaps this is hardly surprising since Ho alone had a wide experience of politics on both the national and international planes. The others knew little of the outside world and had spent their political lives inside Vietnam.

Since 1940 Ho Chi Minh has devoted the whole of his time and energy to the direction of the Communist cause inside former French Indochina, and his achievements speak for themselves. From a small party composed entirely of Vietnamese the Indochinese Communist Party developed rapidly to seize and maintain control of the Vietnamese resistance movement against French rule and spread its tentacles into Laos and Cambodia; it drove France out of Indochina, and today it rules North Vietnam. The name "Indochinese" was abandoned by the party so as to avoid offense to the national susceptibilities of Laos and Cambodia, and three purely national Communist parties were formed. However, the direction of all three parties is provided by the Vietnamese Communists whose declared intention is to re-form a single Communist Party for Vietnam, Laos, and Cambodia when the situation is favorable.[3]

[3] Directive of the Lao Dong Party, dated Nov. 1, 1951, classified "Top Secret." It was captured by the French Expeditionary Corps in North Vietnam during the spring of 1952. See Chapter 6 for further discussion.

Communism is now represented in the "neutral" government of Laos and continues to advance in Cambodia while the government of South Vietnam is fighting for its existence against Communist insurgents directed from Hanoi. The startling progress made by communism in Indochina since 1940 is a measure of Ho Chi Minh's very great political ability. However, he is now in his seventies, and the heavy weight of his responsibilities must soon become too much for him. What of the men who are likely to succeed him?

PHAM VAN DONG

DRV Premier and member of the Politburo Pham Van Dong was introduced to communism by Ho Chi Minh in 1925. A former schoolteacher and journalist, he worked hard to promote the interests of the Indochinese Communist Party, often at the risk of his life, and played a prominent part in directing party affairs until the end of the Second World War. From 1945 onward he devoted his energies increasingly to governmental matters and administration, allowing his purely party activities to decline. Available information does not reveal whether he adopted this course on the orders of Ho Chi Minh or because of his own personal inclinations. Unlike some of his Politburo colleagues, Pham Van Dong has avoided factional strife and personal feuds. Indeed, he has joined Ho Chi Minh in resolving such disputes on more than one occasion and maintains outwardly friendly relations with all the other leaders. Should a power struggle develop in the DRV leadership, Dong is probably the only leader to whom none of the rival factions would take exception. Moreover, he has acquired more experience than the rest in the everyday tasks of running the government and administering the country.

Against these advantages must be set the fact that since Dong has not built up a body of support for himself within the party and enjoys little influence in the army he would be unlikely to become the national leader over the heads of those who command such support. It is more probable that he would survive a conflict for power and subsequently be invited by the victor to serve the new government in a senior capacity, for he could bring to it the benefits of his long experience in administration. Despite his hard struggle and sufferings during the early part of his career, Dong is no political extremist but rather a cautious moderate. His conduct of the Geneva negotiations in 1954 is said to have impressed the Soviets, and he himself is inclined to favor the current policies of Moscow rather than Peking, but he is too prudent publicly to commit himself to one or the other. In private conversations he is sometimes less guarded and has expressed the wish that France had offered Vietnam the same terms which General de Gaulle accorded to Algeria. If she had, he added, then North Vietnam would not be in her present unhappy predicament. He has also stated that he believes Asia's problems can be solved only through cooperation with the white races. Regardless of his personal opinions, however, Dong is hardly likely to impose them upon his colleagues, for he has always accepted the over-all policy decisions of Ho Chi Minh and has directed his own efforts to putting them into practice. Intelligent, thoughtful, hard-working, and sometimes inclined to arrogance toward his subordinates, Pham Van Dong is essentially a follower rather than a leader. If his past may be taken as a guide to his future conduct, then he will continue to rely upon some forceful character to make the major decisions concerning DRV policy.

VO NGUYEN GIAP

One such person is Deputy Premier, Minister of Defense, Commander of the Vietnamese People's Army, and Politburo member Vo Nguyen Giap, a thrusting, outspoken man who is subject to violent emotions, the strongest of which is hatred. Now in his early fifties, Giap became a history teacher after graduating in law at Hanoi University and subsequently emerged as a leader of the Indochinese Communist Party. His obsession with the study of history, which dominated his early life, engendered in him a boundless pride in Vietnam and the Vietnamese people coupled with a deep resentment of what he considered the injustices suffered by his country in the past. For reasons that will be immediately apparent to anyone familiar with Vietnamese history, the resentment was directed primarily against China, but it also kindled in Giap a bitter indignation over the treatment of Vietnam by her French masters. It is interesting to note in passing, and perhaps significant, that the historical character for whom he has always expressed the greatest admiration is Napoleon Bonaparte. His personal friends feel that he tends to identify himself with Napoleon. His indignation over wrongs to the Vietnamese and the vision of himself as a great military leader drew him naturally into revolutionary activities at an early age, as a result of which he was arrested and imprisoned.

Already a leader of the Indochinese Communist Party

at the outbreak of the Second World War, Giap fled
to China, where he joined Ho Chi Minh, and he later
created a guerrilla force in the mountains of northern
Tonkin. When his wife and her sister died in a French
prison after being arrested for their political activities,
he became the implacable enemy of France and conceived so intense a hatred for all things French that it
easily sustained him even in the most difficult periods
of the Indochinese war. So unrestrained and impas-
sioned were his outbursts during the Dalat Conference
of 1946 that Ho Chi Minh felt obliged to omit him
from the Viet Minh delegation to the subsequent
negotiations at Fontainebleau. During Ho's absence in
France it was Giap who governed North Vietnam,
where his ruthless conduct antagonized both Vietnamese
nationalist and foreign opinion. However, his brilliant
direction of the war and his dramatic victory at Dienbienphu made him a hero in the eyes of the Vietnamese
people, second in prestige and popularity only to Ho Chi
Minh in 1954. This very popularity appears to have
made him enemies inside the DRV leadership who are
determined to reduce his importance. His career since
the end of the war has been erratic. At times he has
been eclipsed, and he has twice disappeared completely
from public view for months on end, once in 1957 and
again in 1960. Nevertheless, he has always contrived to
come back again and to retrieve his apparently waning
authority.

ANTAGONISM BETWEEN VO NGUYEN GIAP AND TRUONG CHINH

Of all the enemies Giap has made through his popularity, his forceful behavior, or outspoken comment, the

most formidable opponent, against whom he has conducted a vendetta lasting many years, is Truong Chinh. The latter concentrated his energies upon party work and built up a powerful following within the Lao Dong Party, of which he became Secretary-General. Giap resisted his efforts to impose a tight system of party control upon the army and to add that body to his own growing empire, but he was obliged to make important concessions to Chinh. In 1949 Giap refused to admit that political commissars were necessary in the army, but it was Chinh who prevailed, and by the end of the war the power of the military political commissars was very great indeed. Again, when Chinh argued that communism recognized no national boundaries and urged overt Chinese participation in the fighting, Giap, ever suspicious of Chinese intentions, declared that under no circumstances would the Chinese be allowed to fight in Vietnam. China supplied arms, specialist soldiers, and military advisers, but her participation remained clandestine.

The feud took a more serious turn in 1950 when Chinh accumulated sufficient evidence to secure the execution of Tran Chi Chau, chief of Giap's military supply service and a personal friend of the general. He then repeatedly accused Giap of insecurity in his choice of personnel and provoked quarrels of such violence that all of Ho Chi Minh's and Pham Van Dong's tact and authority were required to avoid a major split in the leadership. Giap's prestige suffered an important setback during 1955 when Chinh and his supporters contrived to reorganize the Ministry of Defense into three branches, the General Staff, the Political Department, and the Supply Department. In his capacity of Minister of Defense Giap was nominally responsible for all of them, but in practice his effective authority was confined to the General Staff, the Political Department being controlled by one of Chinh's appointees and the Supply Department remaining more or less autonomous. Later, in September 1959, the head of the Political Department, Nguyen Chi Thanh, was promoted to the rank of general equal in seniority with Giap himself, and rumors — almost certainly inspired by Chinh — began to circulate in North Vietnam suggesting that Thanh was an abler general than Giap. The vendetta undoubtedly became increasingly bitter following this insult, but no outward signs of it were discernible until a decree of March 15, 1961 stripped Nguyen Chi Thanh of his military rank and transferred him to the task of directing agricultural collectivization. He was replaced in the Ministry of Defense by a less senior officer loyal to Giap, whose position appeared to have been fully restored.

Giap has never made any secret of his distrust and dislike of the Chinese, and this must have been the principal cause of some of his setbacks since any signs of preferment for him cannot but be resented in China. Ho Chi Minh has retained him in the DRV leadership up to the present, but if events ever lead North Vietnam into the Chinese-led camp, then Giap's position will cease to be tenable. Conversely, should Giap emerge as Ho's successor, he is certain to align the country with the Soviet Union and to derive no small satisfaction from participating in Soviet attacks on China. Indeed, at the present time he is restrained only with difficulty by Ho himself, and the speech that he made at Hanoi during the visit of a Chinese military delegation in December 1961 was a model of studied rudeness to the Chinese.

Two factors contribute to Vo Nguyen Giap's strength within the DRV leadership: the loyalty of the army to him and his personal prestige among the Vietnamese people. His principal weaknesses are Chinese enmity and the lack of an organized body of support within the Lao Dong Party. The man's limitless ambition and the vision which he cherishes of himself as an outstanding politico-military leader are sufficient assurance that he will struggle hard to succeed Ho Chi Minh as undisputed leader of the DRV regime.

TRUONG CHINH

Truong Chinh, on the other hand, relies for his importance upon the strength that he commands within the Lao Dong Party, upon a number of powerful figures within the leadership — men such as Hoang Quoc Viet, Nguyen Duy Trinh, Nguyen Chi Thanh — who are closely allied with him, and upon the support of China. Although he was a founding member of the Indochinese Communist Party, Chinh did not rise to the top rank of leaders until 1941, the year when he first met Ho Chi Minh. The latter was so impressed by his ability that he appointed Chinh Party Secretary-General in that same year, a post which he continued to hold throughout the Indochinese war. During the long struggle he had plenty of opportunity to familiarize himself with Chinese communism through the many Chinese who came to Vietnam to assist the resistance movement and through the masses of Chinese political material which were translated into Vietnamese and republished. The more he learned, the more impressed he was with the way things were done in China. From the purely doctrinal point of view his attitude was irreproachable; moreover, many held that Chinese experience was likely to prove more valuable to Vietnam than that of the Soviets because of the many similarities between conditions in Vietnam and China. Only those people who still entertained Vietnam's traditional mistrust of China — a group comprising the entire Vietnamese people with the exception of the most fanatical doctrinaire Communists — could possibly object to Truong Chinh's behavior.

Throughout the Indochinese war Chinh consolidated his position within the Lao Dong Party and insinuated men loyal to him into the other institutions of the state. At the time of the armistice in 1954 his position appeared to be unassailable because, although he was still virtually unknown to the Vietnamese people, his supporters were firmly entrenched in the party organization and held key posts throughout the administration and the armed forces. Well pleased with his success, Chinh continued to advocate the slavish imitation of Chinese policies, and Ho Chi Minh gave his assent. The agrarian reform campaign was carried out under the supervision of Chinese cadres familiar with the similar campaign in China, and Truong Chinh identified himself publicly with it. He thrust the campaign down people's throats, using every available propagandist device, and it was carried out with a brutality and disregard for justice that shocked the Vietnamese peasants more than the war itself had done. Chinese patterns had to be followed even when they proved to be unworkable in the different conditions of Vietnam, and the number of casualties appalled the most battle-hardened soldiers. Hundreds of thousands of patently guiltless people were done to death in the most cruel fashion *"pour décourager les autres*" until the breaking point was reached and outraged peasants, armed only with agricultural tools, rebelled against their new masters in many places throughout the country. Even the loyalty of the army was in doubt, and the whole Communist regime was seriously threatened. Ho Chi Minh hurriedly commenced a "correction of errors" campaign, but the people would not be appeased. They demanded the punishment of the guilty, and the man who was associated with the campaign more than any other was Truong Chinh.

The Lao Dong Party itself was threatened, and Ho was obliged to act quickly if he were not to see the whole of his lifework destroyed. Truong Chinh was forced to resign his post of Secretary-General and to make a public self-criticism, being replaced by Ho himself in an effort to shore up the collapsing authority of the party with his own personal prestige. In this crisis it became apparent that the Vietnamese people were perfectly aware of which leaders wielded power and which were mere puppets, for Nghiem Xuan Yem, the impotent Minister of Agriculture, remained in office, while Ho Viet Thang, the Deputy Minister who controlled the Ministry and was a creature of Chinh, was dismissed. The affair would certainly have ended Truong Chinh's political career but for one thing, the support that he enjoyed from the Chinese Communists. He was a source of acute embarrassment to the DRV Communist leadership, but he could not be removed for fear of adverse Chinese reaction. So, after a period of relative inactivity, he began to fight his way back again and, thanks to the powerful body of support he had built up within the party hierarchy and to his Chinese allies, he is today once more a very powerful figure. However, although he currently occupies third position in the Politburo, it is apparent that his influence within the party is waning and that his activities fall increasingly in the field of government and administration, a phenomenon which could well be the result of Le Duan's work, the present First Secretary of the Lao Dong Party.

LE DUAN

Le Duan, a man of part Chinese extraction, is one of the founder members of the Indochinese Communist Party, but little is known about him since he has concerned himself primarily with clandestine Communist activity and internal party organizational work. He was a leader of the guerrilla war against the French in Cochin China until 1951, when he was recalled to Tonkin and subsequently evaded all publicity until the end of the war. When Ho replaced Truong Chinh as Secretary-General of the party, it was Le Duan who carried out these duties for Ho, but he was not himself appointed to the post officially until 1960, when the title was changed to the Soviet-style First Secretary.

One of the few revealing incidents in the career of Le Duan was his celebrated quarrel with Le Duc Tho, who had been sent to Cochin China in the capacity of Inspector and was an official delegate from the DRV government. The two disagreed about the conduct of the war in the South, and their quarrel became so embittered that it virtually split the southern resistance movement into two mutually hostile camps. In 1951 Le Duan was summoned to Tonkin and Le Duc Tho stayed behind to direct the resistance movement. Both men are now members of the Politburo, and there is little doubt that the enmity between them still persists, but it is carefully concealed in the interests of preserving a façade of unity.

There has been much speculation concerning the strength of Le Duan and the extent of his control over the party, but so little reliable information about him is available that it is impossible to draw any hard-and-fast conclusions. The following, very briefly set out, are the most plausible of the different hypotheses:

1. Le Duan has had more experience directing guerrilla warfare in South Vietnam than the other DRV leaders. Moreover, his appointment as Party First Secretary quickly followed the change of Communist strategy in the South. He was appointed First Secretary for the purpose of directing the war in the South and mobilizing the resources of the party to this end. When victory is achieved, he will be replaced in his party post.

2. Truong Chinh's past disgrace and personal unpopularity in Vietnam make it impossible for him to resume his old party post. This is nominally held by Le Duan, but it is Truong Chinh who controls and directs the latter. At some future date, when the agrarian reform has become no more than a faint memory from the past, Truong Chinh will dispense with his proxy and resume his party functions.

3. Le Duan is inclined to support the Soviet cause in the Sino-Soviet dispute. For that reason he has been appointed to the post of Party First Secretary in order to counterbalance the already great influence of Truong Chinh in the Politburo. Since his appointment he has been engaged in removing Truong Chinh's nominees from their key positions in the party and replacing them with men loyal to himself.

It is impossible to say which, if any, of these three is correct. All that can be stated is that any ambitious man appointed Party First Secretary would be strongly tempted to consolidate his own position and to remove persons loyal to his predecessor from the more important offices. If Le Duan is in fact engaged in doing this, it would offer an explanation for Truong Chinh's gradual dropping of party offices in favor of governmental ones. In any event it would be surprising if no rivalry existed between the dismissed Truong Chinh and Le Duan, and any such rivalry would tend to push Le Duan into the anti-Chinese or pro-Soviet camp.

OTHER POLITBURO MEMBERS

The known enemy of Le Duan in the Politburo, Le Duc Tho, is scarcely likely to be able to create a strong position for himself in the party during Le Duan's tenure of office. The most probable guess is that he allies himself with a faction opposed to Le Duan, possibly that of Truong Chinh. Nguyen Duy Trinh has made it clear on numerous occasions that he is a close ally of Truong Chinh and supports his pro-Chinese stand. Of the remaining Politburo members, two are neither the protégés of others nor *ex officio* members. The first, Le Thanh Nghi, concerns himself almost exclusively with the industrialization of North Vietnam, and the second, Hoang Van Hoan, is the party's foremost expert on external affairs and international negotiations. The fact that the former was selected to accompany Pham Van Dong on a tour of East Europe in mid-1961, one of whose objects was to undo the damage done by Nguyen Duy Trinh's pro-Chinese speeches there a few months earlier, suggests that he is a protagonist of the Soviet Union and for that reason *persona grata* in the countries visited. He is therefore likely to favor Vo Nguyen Giap, Pham Van Dong, and the other pro-Soviet leaders and to be less close to the pro-Chinese Truong Chinh. Hoang Van Hoan has so far successfully avoided committing himself publicly on Sino-Soviet differences.

OTHER LEADERS

Other DRV leaders, while not full members of the Politburo, have built for themselves positions of very considerable strength. Tran Quoc Hoan, for example, is responsible for security and internal order. He controls sizable forces who regularly carry arms, and he is in possession of information concerning all important people in North Vietnam acquired in connection with his security duties. Hoang Quoc Viet, one of Truong Chinh's oldest friends and collaborators, is responsible for all trade union matters.

From this brief survey it will be apparent that the DRV leadership, for all its outward appearance of concord and unanimity, is riven with factional strife, conflicting ambitions, and personal rivalries. However, North Vietnam is a Communist state, and all its major policy decisions are taken by the Chairman of the party and President of the government, Ho Chi Minh. It is impossible to say to what extent these decisions are influenced by individual leaders or factions, but the evidence available suggests that it is very little. There is no question of collective leadership, and Ho Chi Minh appears to be swayed principally by the immediate needs of North Vietnam in her internal and external policies.

Since Ho enjoys immeasurably more popular esteem inside Vietnam than any of the other leaders and has afforded copious proof of his superior political abilities, this situation will probably continue until his death or voluntary retirement. When Ho eventually quits the Vietnamese political scene, a power struggle between rival factions would appear inevitable, the outcome of which it is still too early to predict.

FROM CHINESE DEPENDENT TO COMMUNIST NEUTRAL

3

THE WAR AGAINST FRANCE

The Democratic Republic of Vietnam was officially proclaimed by Ho Chi Minh on September 2, 1945, but since its provincial government lacked all the attributes normally associated with government it is hardly realistic to regard this as the date of its effective establishment. At that time Ho's authority extended over only a small part of Tonkin, and even this was disputed by the nationalist parties. In December 1946, however, it was Ho who ordered hostilities to commence against the French forces, and he was followed into the countryside by both Communists and nationalists. Until late in 1949 Vietnamese resistance continued as a coalition of these groups, but the approach of a Communist victory in China emboldened the Communists to impose their own control upon the movement. A Vietnamese delegation attended the Asian and Australasian Trade Union

Conference at Peking in November 1949 and returned with directives from the Chinese Communists. In Vietnam the Federation of Labor held the first national conference of trade unions for the purpose of implementing the decisions of the Peking meeting. Among those who attended were Truong Chinh and Hoang Quoc Viet, and the latter was elected Chairman of the newly formed Central Committee of the Federation of Labor. Propaganda and official statements assumed an unmistakably Communist character at about that time, and the resistance movement identified itself with communism. Confirmation of the political shift was supplied in January 1950 when China first and then the Soviet Union accorded official recognition to the North Vietnam Communist government.

Vietnamese resistance to the reimposition of French rule had won a large measure of international sympathy, and France, exhausted by the Second World War, was finding it increasingly difficult to continue support for her flagging forces in Indochina. Indeed, there was a real possibility that the Vietnamese might have won their independence from France unaided, but Ho Chi Minh decided otherwise. A man of Ho's intelligence and political experience could not but have known that to transform a nationalist resistance movement into a militant Communist body would be certain to result in the supply of United States military aid to France. America would provide such assistance not to rob the Vietnamese of national independence, for American sentiment was strongly anticolonialist, but to fight the spread of communism in Asia. And once the United States was committed, China could scarcely stand aside.

The consequence of Ho's decision was involvement of

both the United States and Communist China in the Indochinese war, thereby increasing the scale and significance of the conflict and causing more bloodshed, suffering, and damage to the Vietnamese people. Yet he made the decision without any apparent hesitation. No evidence has yet come to light which would show whether he did so at the insistence of the Chinese Communists or simply to ensure that communism, not nationalism, would emerge the victor in Vietnam. In either case the decision evinced a callous disregard for the sufferings of his own people.

As the war dragged on, Chinese aid to Ho Chi Minh increased greatly. Military advisers, munitions, artillery, medicines, and much else reached Vietnam from China, while Vietnamese troops received training on Chinese soil beyond the reach of their enemies. In addition to this purely military aid, the Vietnamese resistance movement also received political guidance on a very large scale from the Chinese. Translators worked in shifts around the clock translating study documents and propaganda materials from Chinese into Vietnamese.[1] Chinese cadres crossed into Vietnam in large numbers; they advised, lectured, and directed in all parts of the resistance-held territory, while Vietnamese cadres proceeded in thousands to China for political training. The ever-growing Chinese influence proved too much for large numbers of Vietnamese who had supported the resistance struggle from the outset, and those who could manage to do so left the resistance zone in disgust. The remainder swallowed their resentment and accepted Chinese interference as best they could.

[1] See Nhu Phong, "Intellectuals, Writers, and Artists," *The China Quarterly*, No. 9, Jan.–Mar. 1962.

Contacts with the Soviet Union were far fewer, and Soviet aid, which reached the resistance forces only toward the end of the war, was very much smaller than that received from China. For that reason there was nothing remarkable in the fact that the DRV delegation to the International Conference on French Indochina, which met at Geneva in the spring of 1954, maintained very close relations with the Chinese delegation and leaned heavily upon them even for such mundane matters as the supply of food but had comparatively few dealings with the Soviet delegation.

Hoang Van Hoan, the DRV Ambassador to China, was a member of the Vietnamese delegation. Clearly, he and his colleagues felt much more at home with the Chinese in 1954 than they did with the Soviets, who seem to have been regarded as somewhat remote beings — racially, culturally, and geographically far removed from the Vietnamese.

THE RETURN OF PEACE — PREDOMINANT CHINESE INFLUENCE

Following the signature of the armistice agreements and the division of Vietnam into two zones, the DRV leaders devoted their attention to the immediate tasks facing the new Communist state in North Vietnam. If they resented the fact that the Soviet Union had compelled them to accept and sign so unsatisfactory an armistice agreement at Geneva, they showed no signs of this in public; but it is possible that they had been compensated by promises of economic aid. Eight years of war had left immense damage in its wake: almost all the railway lines had been destroyed, roads and bridges

had suffered heavily, large areas of agricultural land left
untilled had become overgrown, the few French-owned
industrial installations were badly run down. The bulk
of the restoration work, at least in its early stages, was
of a fairly elementary nature and did not require highly
trained technicians to complete. China was able to supply the labor foremen, the semiskilled technicians, and
the simple tools necessary for the work, while North
Vietnam supplied the coolie labor. The Chinese also
provided large quantities of rice, cloth, medicines, and
other commodities that were in desperately short supply
in North Vietnam. Chinese aid, indeed, far exceeded the
total aid received from the Soviet Union and the rest
of the Communist bloc put together.

If China provided the major portion of foreign aid to
North Vietnam, she was also the model upon which the
Vietnamese based their own planning and policies. It
is not possible to divine whether the adoption of Chinese
methods was the result of a free choice on the part of
the Vietnamese Communist leadership or whether Chinese economic aid was made conditional upon North
Vietnam's following Chinese patterns. Certainly Truong
Chinh and his collaborators evinced great enthusiasm
for the Chinese way of doing things and threw themselves into the agrarian reform campaign with a fervor
which cannot be doubted, but what of the rest? Vo
Nguyen Giap and his friends are likely to have opposed
any strong Chinese influence simply because it was Chinese. In between these two extremes there must have
been many who hesitated, who entertained doubts about
the wisdom of applying such an extreme measure as
Chinese-style agrarian reform and about permitting
China to exercise so much influence upon Vietnam.

Ultimately it was Ho Chi Minh who made the decision and, whether bowing to strong Chinese pressure or because he considered it best, gave orders to copy China.

Agrarian reform was ruthlessly enforced under Chinese supervision, and a census operation was begun. Private businessmen and traders were stripped of their wealth and their accumulated stocks by deliberately ruinous taxation. Some firms were forced to close their doors; others became joint state–private enterprises. Street traders and most of the artisans were squeezed out of their occupations and considered themselves fortunate if they were able to secure employment as unskilled manual laborers in the war-damage repair projects. Many could find no work and died of starvation, swelling still further the number already killed in the course of the agrarian reform. In the late summer of 1956 yet another Chinese policy, Mao's "Hundred Flowers" campaign, was put into effect in North Vietnam.

Meanwhile, roads were being returned to a usable state by Vietnamese workmen under the supervision of Chinese technicians, some of the most vital bridges were rebuilt, and railway track was being laid. The country was returning to some kind of normalcy, and the time had come for decisions to be taken about the most desirable and profitable direction for future development. Already some of the basic facts of economic life in North Vietnam were impressing themselves upon the minds of the Communist leaders with a painful insistence, and none more than the difficulty of feeding the population. Whatever the plans for developing North Vietnam, they would have to provide sufficient food to keep the people alive and capable of performing useful work. Yet because the DRV was faithfully following the path of China, she had introduced agricultural collectivization, moving rapidly from mutual aid teams to cooperatives, with results which were most disappointing. Despite the vigorous expansion of the area of land under cultivation and the completion of large irrigation projects, it became increasingly obvious that the Vietnamese peasants, like peasants elsewhere, had no love for collectivized agriculture and were not prepared to work so hard in the cooperatives for the profit of the government as they had on their own land for their private advantage. The tasks of maintaining dikes around rice fields, of manuring the fields, of pest eradication, and so on were skimped or neglected. Worse still, the peasants were unwilling to sell the fruits of their work to the government at the unrealistic prices officially laid down.[2] Instead they sold rice, meat, and vegetables on the black market or concealed their produce from the government cadres and retained it for their own consumption. Yet another complicating factor was the rapid rise in the birth rate, which meant more mouths to share an already inadequate food supply.

These are some of the factors that influenced the DRV leaders when they evolved development plans for North Vietnam. Events in South Vietnam also played their part, for the United States left no doubt that it was prepared to supply whatever military and economic aid might be necessary to ensure the survival of the anti-Communist government of President Ngo Dinh Diem. So long as Diem remained in office there could be no hope that trade relations would be opened with the South or that Northern coal might be bartered for Southern rice. North Vietnam had to overcome her shortage of food by herself without help from the South,

[2] See Hoang Van Chi, "Collectivisation and Rice Production," *ibid.*

and all signs were that this state of affairs would persist indefinitely. Moreover, China was desperately short of food, and agricultural difficulties were chronic throughout the Communist bloc. It was therefore decided that North Vietnam should press forward with a rapid and large-scale program of industrialization.

Once the decision to industrialize had been taken, the first problem to be studied was the means for putting the new program into effect. Where were the complex machinery, the technical knowledge, and the highly trained specialists to come from? Assistance of this kind was clearly beyond the resources of China and could be obtained only from the Soviet Union and the more advanced European satellites. By the end of 1956 it must have been obvious to the DRV leaders that the period of Chinese predominance in North Vietnam was nearing its end. The Soviet Union would have to be brought more into the picture. Although such a change in foreign relationships was made imperative by economic needs, there are good reasons for believing that other considerations as well made it welcome. Chinese Communist policies had not only proved unpopular with the people of North Vietnam, they had also proved to be highly unsuccessful. Doubtless, land reform of some kind would have had to be carried through, but the particularly brutal form imposed on the North Vietnamese by the Chinese had inflicted serious damage upon the prestige of the Lao Dong Party and upon the authority of the Communist regime. More antagonisms had been created by the census campaign, and opposition to the regime openly revealed by the "Hundred Flowers" campaign was so strong that it is regarded with some apprehension even today.

THE SWING FROM CHINA
TO THE SOVIET UNION

All Vietnamese, whether Communist or not, must have experienced some misgivings at the presence in North Vietnam of so many Chinese technicians and the very considerable authority they enjoyed. The mere presence of similar numbers of Soviet and East European technicians would have reassured the Vietnamese people and would have tended to reduce Chinese authority. Yet the problem that faced the DRV government was not only to reduce Chinese influence while increasing Soviet and East European influence but to achieve both objectives without impairing good relations with China.

There is no evidence to show how the change was made, but the pattern of DRV behavior suggests the following method: The North Vietnamese probably presented the Chinese with a list of goods and services required to carry out their rapid and ambitious program of industrialization and were told that China was incapable of supplying this help. They then turned to the Soviet Union and the European bloc countries and asked them to provide all the aid needed. A tactic of this kind would have enabled the DRV to make the readjustments they desired without giving the Chinese any pretext for objection. In any event, dependence on China was reduced and Soviet and East European involvement in North Vietnam was increased without generating any apparent Chinese resentment.

The major change in the DRV relationship with the Soviet Union and China took place during 1957, yet the North Vietnamese press and radio gave little indication that such an important switch was taking place.

The new development projects undertaken, more frequent references to Soviet and European technicians, and the economic agreements signed offered some indications of the change but the public attitude of North Vietnam toward China and the Soviet Union remained unaltered. It would have been difficult for an outside observer to detect that North Vietnam was systematically reducing its dependence upon China and introducing greater Soviet participation in her affairs without the evidence of the figures for aid received by North Vietnam from bloc countries. The statistics in Table 3.1 [3] provide the clearest and most conclusive evidence that a major realignment was taking place.

TABLE 3.1 COMMUNIST BLOC AID TO THE DRV
(MILLIONS OF U.S. DOLLARS)

China			Soviet Union and East Europe		
Grants	Credits	Total	Grants	Credits	Total
1955–1957					
200.0	—	200.0	100.0	19.5	119.5
1958–1960					
25.0	75.0	100.0	—	159.0	159.0

During the 1958–1960 period North Vietnam was content to accept what aid China was able and willing to provide, but Soviet and East European aid surpassed that of China both in total amount and in economic importance for North Vietnam's future.

Such a fundamental change in DRV alignment could hardly be effected without major upheavals in the leader-

[3] These figures are taken from William Kaye, "A Bowl of Rice Divided," ibid.

ship, for there were undoubtedly many leaders who had concluded that the DRV's future lay with China and had therefore taken the trouble to cultivate Chinese leaders, confident of a secure base on which to construct their future careers. These men could scarcely be expected to view a switch away from Chinese influence with equanimity. Unless they resisted the move, they risked losing their important positions and being overtaken by men who enjoyed stronger Soviet backing. There is no doubt that an internal struggle of great importance did take place within the Lao Dong Party, but the Vietnamese Communists successfully confined it to their group, and scarcely any evidence leaked out to provide detailed information about the sides taken by individuals or the form which the quarrel took.

On May 12, 1957 a newspaper article by Ton Duc Thang stated that the imminent visit of Soviet President Voroshilov to North Vietnam was a "most important historical event," [4] and no pains were spared to ensure that the visit, which began on May 20, was accorded the maximum publicity. At the end of June it was announced in Hanoi that Ho Chi Minh had decided to make a foreign tour during which he would visit North Korea, Czechoslovakia, Poland, East Germany, Yugoslavia, Hungary, Albania, Bulgaria, and Romania, an itinerary which suggested he might well be seeking aid from the East European satellites.[5] This announcement was followed three days later by the news that Ho intended to depart from Hanoi on July 5, only five days after the first mention of his long tour.[6] Chinese Deputy

[4] *Nhan Dan*, May 12, 1957.
[5] Vietnam News Agency (VNA), June 30, 1957.
[6] *Ibid.*, July 3, 1957.

Minister of Foreign Trade Lin Hai-yun disembarked at Hanoi with a Chinese trade delegation on July 2, and Ho Chi Minh's departure was delayed by 24 hours, ostensibly because of bad weather, although flying conditions over Tonkin appeared perfect. The whole business conveyed an impression of crisis, disorder, and impromptu decisions.

Although the Soviet Union was not mentioned in Ho's itinerary, he spent some time in Moscow in July, at the time when Khrushchev expelled Malenkov, Molotov, and Kaganovich — the "anti-party" group — from the Presidium of the CPSU (Communist Party of the Soviet Union). Ho thus acquired firsthand information about the important changes taking place in the Soviet Union. Meanwhile, a goods exchange and payments agreement was signed at Hanoi between North Vietnam and China in Ho's absence.[7] During August Ho visited Yugoslavia, where relations appear to have been cordial, for President Tito was invited to visit North Vietnam, and the Lao Dong Party newspaper, *Nhan Dan*, published an article entitled "A Heroic People," which was extremely complimentary about Yugoslavia and described her as a "united nation which is building socialism." [8] Clearly, North Vietnam was tightening her links with the Soviet Union, an impression strengthened by an unusually early announcement in Hanoi that the fortieth anniversary of the October Revolution would be celebrated in all parts of North Vietnam over a period of six weeks.[9]

[7] *Ibid.*, July 31, 1957.
[8] *Nhan Dan*, Aug. 1957. (The day of the month has been inadvertently clipped from the author's copy.)
[9] VNA, Aug. 6, 1957.

INTERNAL PARTY CONFLICT

Before returning home Ho Chi Minh spent two days in Peking, where he was greeted effusively, at least four leading newspapers publishing editorials to welcome his arrival. On the same day the Lao Dong Party newspaper in a long article praised the success of the tour and announced that Kim Il Sung, Zawadski, Dieckmann, Tito, and Yugov had accepted invitations to visit North Vietnam.[10] However, when Ho arrived at Hanoi on August 30, the storm had broken inside the Lao Dong Party, and from that moment on developments appear confused to the outside observer. Little information can be gleaned from the newspapers or the radio broadcasts because the conflict was contained within the confines of the party, but one account of it was subsequently published by M. Tongas, a French teacher who had remained in North Vietnam after the Communist takeover and who appears to have had a number of personal friends among the highest echelons of the party. It is not suggested that his account should be accepted without question, for there is no documentary evidence to corroborate it. Nevertheless, pertinent excerpts are included below in English translation because M. Tongas has provided the only available account based on information acquired in Hanoi itself at the time of the events.[11]

The crisis exploded during the visit to Hanoi, in September 1957, of Marshal Voroshilov, President of the Supreme Soviet, and the drama lasted until December 24. It reached such a pitch that in November the disappearance of Ho Chi

---

[10] *Nhan Dan*, Aug. 29, 1957.
[11] Gérard Tongas, *J'ai vécu dans l'enfer communiste au Nord Vietnam et j'ai choisi la liberté* (Paris: Les Nouvelles Editions Debresse, 1961).

Minh from the Vietnamese political scene seemed final and certain.[12] Monster demonstrations had been planned by way of a triumphal welcome for the great Soviet leader. Among others, a mass meeting was arranged in Ba Dinh Square, Hanoi's Red Square. The giant platform erected for the demonstration which had taken place to commemorate the anniversary of the proclamation of the Republic on September 2 had been left in place for this purpose. Spectacular fetes had been fully prepared by a "Committee of Welcome" (I was in touch with some members of this Committee) set up for this purpose. But Voroshilov's arrival was about as welcome as the intrusion of a dog into a game of skittles. So great was the disagreement among the Vietnamese leaders that all the customary pomp and ceremony was canceled. Only one public ceremony took place, the reception at Gialam airport, where some speeches of welcome were made and Voroshilov replied briefly. The rest of the visit passed off in the greatest secrecy. Some days later, on about October 15 [Author's note: It was actually on October 18], a new Russian delegation visited Hanoi, a representative group of the Supreme Soviet. There were very few flags and no public receptions except for one of minimal importance held as a matter of protocol by Dr. Tran Duy Hung, the President of the Hanoi Administrative Committee.

From all appearances — and I received sure confirmation of this later from the very best sources — the flames of dispute really were burning among the Vietnamese leaders and their beloved Lien Xo (Soviets). This resulted in the departure of Ho Chi Minh, under the most extraordinary circumstances, to participate in the celebration of the fortieth

[12] No corroboration for the visit of Marshal Voroshilov in September has been found by the author, and it seems unlikely on the face of it that he should have returned so soon after his visit in May. However, it has been established that he was absent from Moscow during the period in question. Yugoslav Vice-President Vukmanović-Tempo arrived in Hanoi on September 1, but his visit was a little too early to be confused with a visit by Voroshilov. If, however, Voroshilov did visit North Vietnam as M. Tongas says, the fact that no publicity was given to his visit by press and radio would accord with M. Tongas' account of the visit.

anniversary of the October Revolution in the Soviet Union, accompanied by ten or so members of the Lao Dong Party. He left in conditions of the utmost secrecy, without even the attendance at the airport of the diplomatic corps. Not a single minister or well-known personage who was not a member of the party went out to the airport.[13] My questions concerning this strange departure, which had about it the appearance of fleeing, received the answer that Ho Chi Minh had gone to Moscow "in a personal capacity" and not "as Head of State." This was a very poor explanation why the honors to which he was entitled had not been accorded to him, especially when his return was to be greeted with great pomp and the customary ceremonial.

In the interval between his departure and return — he was absent for roughly two months — the drama reached its highest peak. The Vietnamese leaders, always deeply divided among themselves over the question of relations with foreign states, were split even more profoundly during that period. While some extolled the indestructible friendship with the Soviets, others advanced the cause of Chinese friendship. Thus it was that at the very paroxysm of the crisis the pro-Chinese carried the day and boycotted the pro-Soviet friendship demonstrations. Ho Chi Minh, seeking continuing friendship with these two powerful allies without submission to either, and the protagonist of a policy of fence-sitting between the Soviet Union and China, left for Moscow alone. His rivals in Hanoi had no wish at all to talk about his actions and gestures during his absence abroad and, to mark the celebration of the fortieth anniversary, did nothing more than organize a bicycle race around Small Lake and show a few Soviet films. This fell very far short of the grandiose celebrations for which we had been waiting. Moreover, from November 10 on the DRV press and radio made no mention of Ho Chi Minh, and this unaccustomed silence was destined to last until his return on December 24.

Everyone soon began to speculate about what had hap-

---

[13] A DRV delegation of 25, led by Hoang Quoc Viet, had already left Hanoi for Moscow on October 18 to participate in the celebration of the fortieth anniversary of the October Revolution.

pened. Many affirmed that he was dead. The circumstances of his mysterious demise were accorded varying explanations and commentaries. Some maintained that he had died somewhere in Siberia, purged by the Soviets, while a double was standing in for him at the receptions in the Soviet Union. Others held that he had left Hanoi seriously ill and intended going to the Soviet Union for medical treatment, but that he had been dead when he arrived in Peking and the Chinese had returned his corpse to Hanoi immediately. There it had been embalmed in the greatest secrecy. All these rumors — nobody knew their origins — achieved a very wide circulation, and the cadres, who were well aware of them but themselves had no information concerning the President, did not know what to say or what sort of attitude to adopt.

During all this time a hectic exchange of letters was going on. Ho Chi Minh, in full disagreement with Hanoi, laid down his minimum conditions and refused to return unless he had first received full satisfaction. It is significant that he spent a month's "holiday" at Hankow. Then he waited until the commemoration of December 19 and the anniversary of the foundation of the Vietnamese People's Army [VPA], celebrated on December 22, had passed before he commenced his journey home. He arrived back in the capital only on December 24, and he did not send his customary Christmas greeting to the Catholics any more than he had done for the occasions of December 19 or 22. [Note by M. Tongas: "It had always been his custom at this time of the year to send a message on December 19 to Dr. Tran Duy Hung, President of the (Hanoi) Administrative Committee, and to General Vuong Thua Vu, the two instigators of the Hanoi uprising on December 19, 1946; and on December 22 he used to send another to Vo Nguyen Giap to mark the formation of the Vietnamese People's Army in that same year."] These three extremely important omissions — they were most untypical of his own habits and of those of the regime — were everywhere remarked upon and indicated a discernible change of attitude.

It must be recorded that the rumors about Ho Chi Minh which had received such a wide circulation, far from saddening the people, rather rejoiced their hearts that at least one of their tyrants had disappeared.

That is how the events of the fall and winter of 1957 appeared to a resident of Hanoi who enjoyed the elevated status of "foreign technician" and who boasted the acquaintance, if not the friendship, of senior members of the Lao Dong Party. Parts of the narrative, such as the second visit of Voroshilov, are puzzling, and there is a slight error — a matter of three days — in one of the dates, but the absence of press and radio mention of Ho Chi Minh has been found to be correct. Undoubtedly there is some truth in the account, and I entertain no doubts about the honesty and integrity of M. Tongas, whom I have met. It offers an explanation for the most curious behavior of the DRV leaders during the period in question. The reader must decide for himself how much of it should be accepted. An additional piece of evidence, which M. Tongas appears not to have noticed, was the failure of the DRV press and radio to mention the name of General Vo Nguyen Giap, the most pro-Soviet of the DRV leaders, during the whole period of Ho Chi Minh's absence. He was, however, mentioned the day following the return of the President. General Giap had not been a member of either of the DRV delegations that visited Moscow, and there is no record of his having left North Vietnam. His whereabouts during this momentous period remain a matter for speculation.

M. Tongas also failed to mention the one public meeting held in Hanoi for the visiting delegation from the Supreme Soviet, yet this omission too is revealing. The order of the DRV leaders on the platform was one that had never been witnessed before and has not been repeated since. The first place was occupied by the senile Vice-President Ton Duc Thang, which appears reasonable since President Ho Chi Minh was abroad, but the second and third places were occupied by Truong Chinh and Nguyen Duy Trinh and the fourth by Pham Van Dong. Now Pham Van Dong, the Premier, ought to have outranked Truong Chinh and Nguyen Duy Trinh since they are only Vice-Premiers; moreover Dong outranks Trinh in the Politburo of the Lao Dong Party. The principal speech was delivered by Nguyen Duy Trinh, and its content was singularly ill-chosen for a speech on a Soviet anniversary before a Soviet delegation unless it was the speaker's intention to insult them, for he quoted extensively from the works of Mao Tsetung.

In Moscow the Declaration and Peace Manifesto were proclaimed, and the DRV delegation returned to Hanoi on November 28 without Ho Chi Minh. Le Duan made his report on the Moscow meeting to the Party Central Committee on December 4, and the documents were formally approved the following day by the DRV government, the Standing Committee of the National Assembly, and other bodies. Addressing a meeting of officials on December 7, Le Duan stated:

The Moscow documents have not only confirmed the line and created favorable conditions for North Vietnam to advance toward socialism but have also shown the path of struggle for national liberation and have created favorable conditions for the revolutionary movement in South Vietnam.[14]

[14] VNA, Dec. 7, 1957.

It is difficult to assess the events that took place in North Vietnam during the latter half of 1957 and to place them in their true perspective. Certainly differences existed between the Soviet Union and China at the time, but Mao Tse-tung appears to have recognized the necessity for unity within the Communist bloc and the need for a single leader of the bloc. From all the available evidence he seemed quite prepared to allow the Soviet Union to be that leader, with the proviso that it provide the right kind of leadership. For this reason it would be wrong to view what happened in North Vietnam in the same light as the same events would have to be viewed had they occurred in early 1963. There can be little doubt that the DRV leadership was sharply divided and that Ho Chi Minh's position was challenged, but the reasons are probably to be found in the personal rivalries which existed between individual leaders, their relations with one another and with Chinese and Soviet leaders, and their personal ambitions as much as in the points of dispute between the Soviet Union and China. The fact that the crisis came about at the very moment when North Vietnam made the decision to replace predominantly Chinese aid by predominantly Soviet and East European aid can scarcely be attributed to coincidence. More probably the crisis was brought to a head by that important reorientation and its effects upon existing dissensions within the leadership. But wherever the truth may lie, the return of Ho Chi Minh to Hanoi on December 24, 1957 and the reappearance of Vo Nguyen Giap offer convincing proof that differences had been resolved, the crisis averted, and a compromise solution, however temporary, reached.

PARTY UNITY RESTORED

A mark of the renewed stability in the DRV leadership was Ho Chi Minh's decision to visit India and Burma during February 1958, and his confidence was not misplaced, for all appeared to run smoothly during the early months of that year. New trade agreements were signed with the Soviet Union and China during March and April, while a middle-of-the-road political line was followed, with Premier Pham Van Dong informing the National Assembly that North Vietnam supported the Soviet initiative in stopping nuclear tests unilaterally and also supported the Chinese people's struggle to liberate Taiwan and smash the United States conspiracy to create two Chinas.[15] If the swing toward greater reliance upon the Soviet Union is reflected in the 26 slogans proclaimed for May Day,[16] none of which referred specifically to China, it would be a mistake to attach too much importance to this. Perhaps the true position is best summed up by the National Assembly Deputy for Phu-yen, Comrade Tran Quynh. In his capacity as spokesman of the National Assembly's Political Subcommittee he said:

Our firm international position is to stand in the socialist camp headed by the Soviet Union. . . . This position proceeds from our people's fundamental interests and from the requirements of North Vietnam's advance towards socialism.[17]

Harmony was first disturbed by Yugoslavia, and the sequence of events was such as to make the DRV leaders

[15] New China News Agency (NCNA), Apr. 16, 1958.
[16] VNA, Apr. 19, 1958.
[17] *Ibid.*, Apr. 27, 1958.

appear a little foolish in the eyes of outside observers, which probably contributed some extra bitterness to the affair. In the latter part of April Tito was re-elected President of Yugoslavia and Popović was reappointed Foreign Minister. President Ho Chi Minh and Pham Van Dong, in his capacity as Foreign Minister, sent a joint cable in which they expressed the hope that Tito and Popović would achieve many new successes in the building of socialism in Yugoslavia.[18] It was unfortunate that only a few days later these high hopes were dashed by the announcement of the Yugoslav Draft Program, which North Vietnam felt obliged to attack. The daily newspaper of the Lao Dong Party published excerpts from an article, "Modern Revisionism Must Be Criticized," which had appeared in the Peking *People's Daily* three days earlier.[19] In its own editorial *Nhan Dan* wrote:

It is regrettable, however, that the position and viewpoints of the authors of that Draft Program have departed from Marxism-Leninism. They are the position and viewpoints of modern revisionism — no more, no less.[20]

There followed an anti-Yugoslav campaign, of which abuse and invective are the most memorable features, and the Yugoslav Ambassador departed from Hanoi at the beginning of July.

Still greater strains were imposed on the DRV leadership by lack of Soviet enthusiasm for China's "Great Leap Forward," for her introduction of communes, and for the flare-up in the Formosa Straits. Hanoi accorded high praise to China's actions, describing Chinese suc-

[18] *Ibid.*, Apr. 23, 1958.
[19] *People's Daily*, May 5, 1958.
[20] *Nhan Dan*, May 8, 1958.

cesses as "the results of the correct leadership of the CCP based on the creative application of Marxist-Leninist basic principles to the practical conditions of China." [21] The communiqué issued after the Khrushchev–Mao Tse-tung talks was loudly acclaimed in North Vietnam, but Vietnamese comment revealed an interpretation of the communiqué very close to China's. Indeed, NCNA quoted speeches made by several DRV leaders.[22] On August 24 the Lao Dong Party's publishing house, Su That, published a book describing the achievements of the Chinese people in the fields of agriculture, industry, culture, and education during the "Great Leap Forward" movement.[23] Throughout September and October full DRV support for China on the question of Taiwan was voiced ceaselessly in the press and radio, and much of it was repeated by NCNA. Even Vo Nguyen Giap, always the most guarded of the DRV leaders in voicing his support for China, threw aside his accustomed reticence when delivering a farewell speech to the Albanian military delegation that had visited North Vietnam under the leadership of Defense Minister Balluku. Both the Vietnamese and Albanian peoples and armies, he said, "are always ready by the side of the CPR [Chinese People's Republic] in its struggle to recover Quemoy and Matsu, and to liberate Taiwan." [24]

Statements of this kind might suggest that North

[21] This quotation was taken from a *Nhan Dan* editorial published on July 1, 1958. It can be paralleled by many others from newspapers, public speeches by DRV leaders, and radio broadcasts.

[22] NCNA on Aug. 4, 1958 quoted from speeches by Hoang Quoc Viet, Tran Huu Duc, and Duong Duc Hien. On Aug. 5, 1958 the same agency quoted from speeches by Ton Duc Thang, Bui Ky, Duong Bach Mai, and others.

[23] NCNA, Aug. 4, 1958.

[24] VNA, Oct. 27, 1958.

Vietnam had moved closer to China than ever before and was wholeheartedly committed to the support of Chinese actions and policies, but such was not the case. Despite the outpouring of words, what actually took place in North Vietnam showed that the DRV had no intention of adopting a "Great Leap Forward" campaign herself and never attempted to introduce communes. In fact, this was the first instance of the DRV technique, later to become familiar, of responding to pressure from the Soviet Union or China by offering verbal support but taking no action. It is very probable, although not a scrap of evidence has so far come to light which would corroborate it, that Ho Chi Minh was secretly reassuring the Soviet leaders, explaining that North Vietnam was supporting China only with empty words, while her actions proved that she had not been taken in by Maoist innovations.

THE DIFFICULT MIDDLE PATH

4

FOLLOWING THE MIDDLE ROAD

While justifying Cambodia's neutralist stand in the struggle going on in the world between East and West, Prince Norodom Sihanouk once said, "When elephants fight, then the ant must stand aside." North Vietnam must feel rather like the ant while the Soviet Union and China struggle against one another, but it is not always possible for her to stand aside. She would seem to have reached the conclusion that the next safest spot is the neutral ground between the combatants, and this is the place she invariably seeks to occupy. However, even an ant has to attend to the running of its anthill. While the two Communist giants are locked in combat, the ant's principal concern is almost certainly for the safety of its anthill and will direct its efforts to ensure that neither combatant damages or destroys its anthill.

This analogy provides a fairly accurate description of

North Vietnam's behavior from late 1958 until the present time. On more than one occasion she has been subjected to pressures from either side, has been cajoled or threatened, has had to face demands from visiting delegates which have sometimes been embarrassing, has had to participate in international Communist meetings, and so on. Throughout she has sought to avoid causing offense to either the Soviet Union or China and at the same time to extract the maximum benefit for North Vietnam from their dispute; but always the primary consideration has been to preserve her own independence and freedom of action. Nevertheless, it should not be forgotten that Ho Chi Minh and his colleagues are Communist political leaders and, like politicians the world over, will spare no effort to remain in power. Any weakening of the Communist bloc would inevitably weaken their own authority in North Vietnam and would encourage their opponents. Consequently, the Vietnamese Communist leadership has a very real interest in upholding the strength of communism in the world, an interest stemming more from personal considerations than ideological conviction. This factor exercises an important influence upon the actions and policies of North Vietnam.

Unlike the previous year, 1958 saw the anniversary of the October Revolution celebrated in North Vietnam with considerable pomp and circumstance. There were mass meetings, addresses by Communist leaders, theatrical performances, film shows, banners, press and radio tributes, and the rest. Pham Van Dong, in his dual capacity as DRV Premier and member of the Politburo, wrote an article for *Nhan Dan* in which he described the Vietnamese August revolution as a "tributary" of the

October Revolution.[1] Later in November the Su That Publishing House produced the first volume of the first edition of Mao Tse-tung's *Selected Works* in Vietnamese, and *Nhan Dan* described Mao's writings as "classics of Marxism-Leninism linked with the practice of the Chinese revolution." The balance was being maintained.

Closer relations with Albania seemed to occupy an important place in the minds of the DRV leadership during the closing months of 1958. In October an Albanian military delegation visited North Vietnam, and its leader, Defense Minister Balluku, made an important speech in Hanoi during the course of which he said, "Although standing at two opposite ends of the socialist camp, Albania and North Vietnam are close to one another in a common struggle against the enemies of Marxism-Leninism and for a socialist life." Referring to imperialist attempts to divide the socialist front and the international Communist movement, he criticized the modern revisionism of the Tito clique, which, he added, has shown itself "very skilled in the service of the US dollar." [2] A protocol on cultural cooperation to implement in 1959 and 1960 the provisions of the long-term cultural agreement, concluded in Tirana the previous year during Ho Chi Minh's visit to Albania, was signed in Hanoi on November 24. The document provided for exchanges of delegations, scholars and students, research material, and literature.[3] In the course of a banquet in honor of Albania's National Day, Premier Pham Van Dong congratulated the Albanian people on their

[1] Quoted by VNA, Nov. 7, 1958.
[2] *Ibid.*, Oct. 23, 1958.
[3] *Ibid.*, Nov. 25, 1958.

achievements and their ceaseless efforts against the plots of imperialists and revisionists.[4]

Meanwhile, to the accompaniment of surprisingly little propaganda, the important business of building up the North Vietnamese economy with the help of foreign aid was proceeding. Chinese technicians began arriving early in August to commence work on the construction of consumer goods enterprises,[5] and the completion of a broadcasting and receiving station for the post office was announced at the end of the same month.[6] In December a protocol was signed with the Soviet Union which provided for an exchange of goods during 1959 70 per cent greater than in 1958.[7] Agreements governing Soviet technical and economic aid to North Vietnam as well as scientific and technical cooperation were signed in March,[8] and trading exchanges with China were increased by mutual consent later that month.[9]

NORTH VIETNAMESE PROBLEMS

Whatever progress was being made in the field of industrialization in North Vietnam — and there is ample evidence that it failed to come up to expectations — the results of the collectivization of agriculture and the imposition of a socialist pattern upon the country made it perfectly plain by 1959 that North Vietnam was showing no signs of achieving economic self-sufficiency. The demands of the North Vietnamese people were not

[4] *Ibid.*
[5] VNA, Aug. 1, 1958.
[6] Hanoi Radio, Aug. 15, 1958.
[7] VNA, Dec. 30, 1958.
[8] *Ibid.*, Mar. 7, 1959.
[9] *Ibid.*, Mar. 20, 1959.

great and did not extend to luxury goods or even to the kinds of consumer goods considered necessities in the more advanced bloc countries. Nevertheless, they required food and clothing, peasants could not work in the fields unless they were enabled to replace worn-out implements, and households demanded a basic minimum of domestic utensils for cooking and eating. It was proving impossible to satisfy even these modest demands, and the major problem was food.

Ho Chi Minh had never entertained any hopes of being able to conclude satisfactory agreements concerning the reunification of Vietnam with President Ngo Dinh Diem, but he clearly hoped — and not without good grounds — that Diem's regime would be overthrown and replaced by a government which would prove more amenable. The first requirement of North Vietnam from South Vietnam was food, for North Vietnam had long been a food-deficit area. By 1959 it had become obvious that, thanks to generous United States aid, President Diem had consolidated his position and had effectively silenced most of the opposition to his regime, and that North Vietnam was not going to obtain any of South Vietnam's food surplus in the foreseeable future unless new methods were adopted. Moreover, hopes of acquiring food from other bloc countries were nonexistent, for agriculture has always been the weakest point of communism, and no bloc country had any surplus for export to North Vietnam.

The desperate and increasing food shortage led the DRV leadership to decide — probably at the meeting of the Central Committee of the Lao Dong Party held in May 1959 — to change its tactics toward South Vietnam and to revert to the technique of the "people's war" that had served so well during the war against France.[10] By using this technique, in which the Vietnamese Communists are the most skillful and experienced practitioners in the world, they hoped to subvert the government of South Vietnam and procure its overthrow while not ostensibly engaging in warfare against that state. The decision was not without risks for both North Vietnam and the entire Communist bloc, but doubtless Ho Chi Minh had discussed the matter with Soviet leaders during his visit to Moscow to attend the Twenty-First Congress of the CPSU and with the Chinese leaders during his stopover in Peking. Thus by the middle of 1959 North Vietnam was committed to the waging of an armed struggle in South Vietnam the objective of which was the overthrow of President Ngo Dinh Diem's regime.

Whatever reactions the fighting in South Vietnam might provoke, it was a war from which disengagement would be difficult. The most important reason is that, once the struggle had begun, any withdrawal would entail the abandonment of North Vietnam's supporters in South Vietnam, who, if abandoned, would not support any subsequent campaign. Thus Ho Chi Minh and his colleagues could not afford to allow any international congress of Communist parties to condemn the waging of local wars. Since the Soviet Union has always shown herself to be more aware than China of the disastrous consequences of nuclear war, or at least has permitted her policies to be more obviously directed toward the avoidance of situations in which there was a risk of

[10] For an excellent description of this type of warfare see George K. Tanham, *Communist Revolutionary Warfare* (New York: Frederick A. Praeger, 1962).

nuclear war, the North Vietnamese decision to wage armed struggle against the authorities of South Vietnam, even if initially approved by the Soviet Union, still contained the risk of possible differences between North Vietnam and the Soviet Union at some future date, particularly if the war went the wrong way for North Vietnam. Signs that such differences were in fact developing became apparent during 1962.

THE MIDDLE ROAD AGAIN

The Twenty-First Congress of the CPSU was attended by Ho Chi Minh himself, and there are many indications that the business of the Congress made a deep impression on the North Vietnamese Communists. On his return to Hanoi, Ho addressed a large open-air meeting and spoke of the "brilliant success" of the Congress and the "great significance" of the Soviet seven-year plan.[11] An important article in the Lao Dong Party theoretical journal, Hoc Tap, emphasized that the Congress had laid down the rules for the transformation to communism when it stated:

In order to achieve communism and practice the principle of distribution according to needs, a transitional stage is indispensable — the socialist phase — in which the ideological and material tasks of communism are systematically secured.[12]

At about the same time Premier Pham Van Dong was voicing his support for the establishment of a nuclear-free zone in the Far East, a policy Khrushchev had

[11] VNA, Feb. 20, 1959.
[12] Hoc Tap, Mar. 1959.

strongly advocated in his speech to the Twenty-First Congress of the CPSU:

The Vietnamese people and the government of North Vietnam warmly approve and fully support Comrade Khrushchev's statement on the need to establish in the Far East and all over the Pacific area a peace zone and, first of all, a zone free from atomic weapons.[13]

Early in July Ho Chi Minh again flew to Moscow,[14] where he remained for almost two months, an exceptionally long absence for a head of state who controls the government and party as closely as Ho. The reason given in the press was that he had gone to spend his summer holiday in the Soviet Union, but the length of his trip and its timing make this statement more than a little doubtful. There is no clue to be found in DRV newspapers or radio broadcasts which would divulge the true reason for the visit, but, since Khrushchev was to visit the United States in September and Ho Chi Minh did not leave the Soviet Union until August 20,[15] it seems likely that the two discussed the Soviet leader's American trip. Undoubtedly Soviet aid to North Vietnam and the commencement of the armed struggle in South Vietnam also featured in their talks. Before returning to Hanoi, Ho spent four days in Peking where he met with Liu Shao-chi, Chou En-lai, Chen Yi, and other Chinese leaders. Once again published and broadcast materials offer no information about what was discussed, but when Ho reached Hanoi on August 25, all outward signs indicated that North Vietnam was successfully

[13] VNA, Mar. 4, 1959.
[14] *Ibid.*, July 3, 1959.
[15] Peking Radio news bulletin, Aug. 21, 1959.

maintaining good relations with both the Soviet Union and China.

Chinese anger was stirred by Khrushchev's visit to the United States and particularly by his talks with Eisenhower at Camp David. There can be little doubt that the principal reason for his sudden decision to visit Peking to attend the celebrations for the tenth anniversary of the Communist regime was to placate Mao and the other Chinese leaders. Despite the very strained atmosphere in China at the time, or more probably on account of it, Ho Chi Minh also attended these celebrations in person, and the role he played was that of the conciliator. In public he praised Mao and the CPR, saying "Vietnam and China are two brother countries having close relations like lips and teeth," [16] but this was after all a Chinese anniversary. Behind the scenes he probably played an important part in allaying the mutual suspicion and antagonism that existed between Khrushchev and Mao.

North Vietnam celebrated the 1959 Chinese anniversary with all the usual ceremonies but added a program of specially organized talks on the Chinese people's "Great Leap Forward," held in all parts of the country, and published in Vietnamese some works by Mao and other Chinese writers.[17] Three weeks later a similar program was prepared for the forty-second anniversary of the October Revolution, the theme for the talks on that occasion being "Helping Vietnamese to Understand Better the Historic Lessons of the Revolution." [18] These were intentionally transparent tactics to demon-

[16] NCNA, Sept. 29, 1959.
[17] VNA, Sept. 27, 1959.
[18] *Ibid.*, Oct. 23, 1959.

strate to both the Soviet Union and China that North Vietnam did not wish to be dragged into a dispute by either side but wanted to maintain friendly relations with both.

Impartiality remained the constant factor in all DRV actions and pronouncements during the following months. November saw *Nhan Dan* defending in a long editorial "the Soviet Union's unswerving policy of peace and peaceful coexistence" [19] and a week later celebrating the fifteenth anniversary of Albanian liberation. Even the eightieth anniversary of Stalin's birth, though it must have taxed Vietnamese ingenuity, did not find them wanting, and the lengthy *Nhan Dan* article[20] on that occasion was a masterpiece of diplomacy. After describing him as an outstanding leader of the revolutionary workers' movement in the Soviet Union and the world, of the CPSU and the Soviet state, and an outstanding theoretician of Marxism-Leninism, the paper recalled that Stalin had played a decisive role in the struggle against the White Guards and the foreign interventionists and had showed a firm resolve to abide by the teachings of Lenin concerning the line of socialist construction in the Soviet Union. Stalin's errors in later life were set out, but only in order to demonstrate how the CPSU, with "great determination and courage," had corrected them and achieved "splendid results." Khrushchev's announcement of cuts in the Soviet armed forces was hailed as proof of his determination to achieve peace, and a full measure of indignation was expressed over the U-2 affair.

[19] *Nhan Dan,* Nov. 22, 1959.
[20] *Ibid.,* Dec. 21, 1959.

SINO-SOVIET DIFFERENCES

Differences between the Soviet Union and China became more acute in the early summer of 1960 and centered around the question of peaceful coexistence. In May Khrushchev heaped scorn on rumors that "other socialist countries" were demanding that the Soviet Union abandon her policy of *détente*, and the Soviet press in early June dismissed Chinese criticisms of peaceful coexistence and launched vigorous attacks on "left sectarians." [21] It is possible to assess the degree of bitterness by comparing statements made by the two sides. The Soviet disarmament proposal made on June 2 asserted that the "goal . . . of banishing war from the life of human society altogether" had become practicable, had become possible to achieve.[22] The *People's Daily*, however, stated: "To spread any impractical illusion about peace will only lull the vigilance of the masses," [23] and Liu Chang-shen described the Soviet proposition as an "unrealistic illusion." [24] The Congress of the Romanian party at Bucharest offered an opportunity for a confrontation, and Khrushchev, who attended in person, strongly reasserted the Soviet position and countered the Chinese attacks upon it. Although the Chinese delegate was more restrained in his speech to the gathering, he made it clear that China had no intention of retreating from her position. The communiqué issued at the conclusion of the meeting showed

[21] For typical examples, see *Soviet Russia*, June 10, 1960 and *Pravda*, June 12, 1960.

[22] *Pravda* and *Izvestiya*, June 4, 1960.

[23] *People's Daily*, June 7, 1960.

[24] Speech by Liu Chang-shen, NCNA, June 8, 1960.

every sign of a compromise reached after some hard bargaining, but Chinese and Soviet statements subsequently made it clear that the dispute continued unabated.

North Vietnam generally subscribed to Soviet statements on peaceful coexistence until the meeting of the Warsaw Pact in February 1960, when the true depth of the difference between Soviet and Chinese views seems to have become apparent to the Vietnamese leaders. Thereafter they carefully eschewed favorable comment about peaceful coexistence but with equal care avoided subscribing to the Chinese thesis that condoning the imperialists' "peace tactics" would adversely affect the revolutionary zeal of "peoples' struggles." Conflicting arguments put forward by the Soviet Union and China on the occasion of Lenin's Day in April were completely ignored in North Vietnam, which failed to publish or broadcast statements made by either side. Indeed, the issues of war and peace might not have existed at all, to judge by the contents of *Nhan Dan* and — even more surprisingly — *Hoc Tap*.

It is interesting to note at this point that most foreign observers of Communist affairs had already developed their own techniques for assessing the positions taken by Communist parties other than those of the Soviet Union and China. These generally consisted of studying all the statements of the parties on the most important issue of the moment — in this case the question of peaceful coexistence — and of branding them pro-Soviet or pro-Chinese on the basis of whether they had supported or attacked the contention of either side. Not unnaturally the foreign observers noticed that North Vietnam had supported peaceful coexistence until February 1960 and had then ceased to do so, a phenomenon which was then construed as meaning that North Vietnam had been pro-Soviet until that date and had subsequently transferred her allegiance to China. Without doubt they were correct in their classification of most other parties by this means, but they were assuming that every party must be a supporter of either China or the Soviet Union, and their technique took no account of the possibility that a Communist party might choose to remain neutral or uncommitted. For that reason their assessment of the position of the Lao Dong Party was incorrect and has largely remained so to the present time.

Le Duan, who led the DRV delegation to the Bucharest Congress, witnessed the clash between the Soviet and Chinese viewpoints and must certainly have been aware of the private arguments going on between the two sides over the wording of the final communiqué, yet he adhered steadfastly to the neutral line which his party had elected to follow. Ignoring the major issues of debate, he made a speech devoted entirely to Romanian and Vietnamese affairs. Subsequently *Nhan Dan* published an article on the Romanian Congress reflecting the neutral attitude of North Vietnam but laying some stress on the need for bloc unity.[25] Premier Pham Van Dong's speech to the National Assembly on the same subject was little more than a paraphrase of the final communiqué. That the Lao Dong Party was deeply concerned about the Sino-Soviet differences is indicated by the long delay before it issued its own statement about the Congress, a document which did not appear until August 14. The statement failed to make any

[25] *Nhan Dan*, June 28, 1960.

mention of either revisionism or dogmatism and, like the earlier *Nhan Dan* article, stressed the need for unity, promising that the Lao Dong Party would "do its best to contribute" to the "unity of mind" of bloc parties.[26]

However much the Vietnamese Communists may have wished to avoid taking sides in the Sino-Soviet dispute, the internal situation of Vietnam imposed some restrictions upon the attitudes that it was possible for them to adopt. Because North Vietnam was committed to the armed struggle going on in South Vietnam, the party statement was obliged to limit its remarks about the inevitability of war to the simple pronouncement that there were increasing possibilities of averting *world* war, which made its standpoint very close to that of China. Not only did it refrain from making any mention of peaceful coexistence, but it also omitted the Bucharest communiqué's statement that the struggle for peace was the main task. Curiously enough, the Vietnamese party's statement was reproduced in full in TASS bulletins and published by *Pravda*,[27] but, despite its slight leaning toward the Chinese position, it was completely ignored in China, perhaps as a consequence of Ho Chi Minh's secret visit to Moscow the very day the Lao Dong Party statement was issued.

THE THIRD LAO DONG PARTY CONGRESS AND AFTER

Preparations for the forthcoming Third Congress of the Lao Dong Party were nearing completion at the time of Ho's visit to Moscow, a trip that would have remained unknown to the outside world — but not,

[26] VNA, Aug. 14, 1960.
[27] *Pravda*, Aug. 16, 1960.

one imagines, in Peking — if it had not been for the apparent carelessness of the Hungarian news agency MTI and the newspaper *Népszabadság*, which reported his presence at the Hungarian Exhibition in Moscow on August 15, 1960. Possibly the fact that Ho made no appearances in North Vietnam between August 3 and August 24 would have been noticed, but the reasons for his absence could only have been guessed at. In the light of subsequent events, certainly the most plausible explanation for his secret trip — although of course there is no evidence to prove this is the correct one — is that Ho Chi Minh went to the Soviet Union to conclude an agreement with Khrushchev. Since the behavior of both the Soviet Union and China after the Bucharest Congress suggested that neither was prepared to make concessions to the other, their differences would be hotly disputed at the next Congress, and that chanced to be the Lao Dong Party Congress at Hanoi.

A mark of the rapid deterioration in relations between the Soviet Union and China was the Chinese readiness to embarrass the Soviets in full view of non-Communists. A delegation of Chinese scholars was scheduled to attend the International Congress of Orientalists in the Soviet capital from August 9 until August 16, 1960. The Chinese failed to appear in Moscow and offered no explanation for their absence, leaving the Soviet organizers to explain to the foreign delegates, the great majority of whom were from non-Communist countries, the reasons for the Chinese absence. They had not received even a telegram with a bogus excuse to show to the visitors.

In such circumstances it is reasonable to suppose that Khrushchev would seek to muster the maximum support for the Soviet Union. Since the Vietnamese party had remained neutral at Bucharest, it was necessary for Khrushchev to make a special effort to secure Vietnamese support, particularly since the Vietnamese would be responsible for the organization of the Congress, the agenda, the order of speaking, the reporting of proceedings, and so on. In order to win this support in Hanoi, Khrushchev would have to strike a bargain with Ho Chi Minh whereby he would supply Ho with something he badly wanted.

Ho Chi Minh for his part needed nothing so much as massive aid and technical assistance for North Vietnam's industrialization, which, as became apparent in the five-year plan announced at the Vietnamese Congress, he intended to push forward at a very fast pace. That Khrushchev did promise such aid is indicated by the vast scale of industrialization envisaged by the plan. It is also significant that Mukhitdinov, the leader of the Soviet delegation to the Congress, went to see Ho immediately after his arrival at Gia-lam airport on August 31 and delivered to him a personal letter from Khrushchev, the contents of which have never been disclosed. Speaking at a public meeting in Hanoi on September 1, Mukhitdinov declared the intention of the Soviet government and party to increase Soviet cooperation with North Vietnam, while Vo Nguyen Giap in his address to the Congress said: "At present, economic construction has become the central task of the party." The same theme was repeated in a number of speeches.

Space does not permit a detailed analysis of all the statements made in the course of the Hanoi Congress.[28]

[28] For a fuller account see P. J. Honey, "North Vietnam's Party Congress," *The China Quarterly*, No. 4, Oct.–Dec. 1960.

Since the general pattern of behavior was established at the public meeting on September 1, it will suffice to record briefly what happened that evening. Pham Van Dong's opening speech, for all its caution, moved away from the earlier neutral position of North Vietnam and closer to that of the Soviet Union. In it he stated:

Nowadays the Soviet Union and other socialist countries are successfully building socialism and communism and have become an invincible force. Along with peace-loving people all over the world, they are able to prevent war, to check the bloodstained hands of the imperialists, preserve peace, and save mankind from a new world war, a nuclear war.[29]

Dong went on to define the present era as one of "transition from capitalism to socialism," the Soviet phrase, and did not use the Chinese phrase "imperialism and proletarian revolution." He also praised "the policy of peaceful coexistence of the Soviet Union and the socialist camp" but ignored the proposal for a nuclear-free zone in the Far East and a Pacific peace pact. This omission was particularly significant because Chou En-lai had laid heavy stress upon this proposal during the April meeting of the National People's Congress and China had devoted much publicity to it in the months preceding the Vietnamese Party Congress. The Soviet Union, on the other hand, appeared to have lost interest. In the month of August North Vietnam had on several occasions expressed support for this plan, but now Pham Van Dong failed to make any mention of it.

Mukhitdinov spoke next and stated the Soviet case with some vigor. "The foreign policy of the Soviet Union," he said,

[29] VNA, Sept. 1, 1960.

aims at ensuring a lasting peace among nations, eliminating
the cold war, and ending the armaments race. The policy is
winning warm support from the working people throughout
the world because it reflects their fundamental interests. The
Soviet Union undertakes to create conditions for eliminating
the possibilities of provoking war. The clear and concrete
proposals of the Soviet government on general and complete
disarmament, put forward in various speeches by Premier
Khrushchev, is the correct way to create a favorable atmosphere in international relations.[30]

He was followed by Li Fu-chun, the leader of the
Chinese delegation, who talked of the "comradeship in
arms between the Chinese and Vietnamese peoples" and
devoted the greater part of his speech to reiterating the
various factors which bound China and Vietnam together.

The treatment accorded to these three speakers by
the Soviet, Chinese, and Vietnamese news agencies is
interesting, and it too set a pattern for the reporting of
the Vietnamese Congress. Pham Van Dong's speech
was reported by all three agencies, but NCNA omitted
his references to the possibility of avoiding war. TASS
and VNA reported Mukhitdinov's speech, but NCNA
made no mention of it. NCNA reported Li Fu-chun's
speech in full, but VNA simply named him as a speaker,
giving no details of what he said, although the agency
reported separately on the other main speeches. The
TASS report of the meeting omitted Li Fu-chun altogether. Perhaps the most significant speech was Le Duc
Tho's report on the revision of the party constitution,
in which he launched an outspoken attack on dogmatism,
although he restricted his remarks to the Lao Dong
Party. He said,

[30] *Ibid.*

Dogmatism is quite serious among the leading cadres at all levels. It is most readily observed in the mechanical study and application of foreign experiences. . . . Dogmatism has limited the creative power of the party and the masses, has hampered the development of the wisdom and experience of our whole party.[31]

An analysis of all the Vietnamese speeches made before, during, and after the Hanoi Congress leaves no room for doubt that North Vietnam had shifted its previous position and moved closer to the Soviet Union. It is true that no Vietnamese speaker attacked Chinese policies directly, but this has never been a Vietnamese practice. Indeed, North Vietnam has never directly attacked any other Communist state with the single exception of Yugoslavia. Neither has it ever aligned itself irrevocably with one of the two Communist giants involved in the dispute, for Ho Chi Minh is far too experienced and able a politician to make an elementary mistake of that kind. Instead, its practice has been to accord praise to the policies of one of the parties while saying as little as is consistent with the minimum standards of politeness about the other. Within these characteristic limits of its political behavior, North Vietnam may fairly be said to have swung to the Soviet side in early September 1960. This impression is strengthened by the manner in which VNA reported the Congress. The agency reported Vietnamese and Soviet speakers fully; it devoted less space to Chinese speakers and, on one or two occasions, omitted to report them at all. Soviet attacks on the Chinese positions were faithfully reported while Chinese attacks tended to be edited out.

In retrospect the Hanoi Congress shows every indi-

[31] *Ibid.*

cation of a secret agreement having been concluded between Ho Chi Minh and Khrushchev. Ho had nothing to offer except the support of North Vietnam, and this he appears to have given to the Soviet Union within the limits of political prudence. In return Khrushchev would seem to have offered promises of the technical aid North Vietnam badly needed for her industrialization. It is difficult to understand how North Vietnam could seriously have approved a five-year plan envisaging so vast and rapid an increase in industrial construction unless she had first received assurances of sufficient technical assistance from the Soviet Union to carry it out.

The extent of Chinese isolation during the weeks following the Hanoi Congress was underlined on the occasion of China's National Day, Albania being the only country of the Communist bloc to send a delegation to Peking to participate in the celebrations. For the first time since 1949, *Pravda* failed to publish an editorial commemorating the anniversary, and messages from other bloc countries were noticeably cool, all pointing out to the Chinese the advantages of cooperation. Polite as always, North Vietnam dispatched a message which expressed thanks for Chinese aid, but the whole text evinced a marked lack of enthusiasm and expressed a sentiment no more encouraging than an assurance that China's achievements had "greatly encouraged the national democratic movement."

Although it is possible for able politicians by a judicious choice of words and frequent resorts to ambiguity to leave others in some doubt about the precise meaning of their statements or policies, the practical application of these policies often tends to be uncomfortably revealing. This was a lesson the Vietnamese Communists were learning in the all too practical activity of agricultural collectivization. A recipient of agricultural aid from both China and the Soviet Union, North Vietnam had carried through a Maoist agrarian reform, presumably arguing that the similarity of local conditions in the Vietnamese and Chinese countryside made this most suitable, and had proceeded through the progressive stages of mutual aid teams, low-level cooperatives, and so on. By the late summer of 1960 she found herself in the embarrassing situation of having to reveal to Chinese and Soviet agricultural advisers whether or not she proposed to copy the model of the Chinese communes. The avoidance of the term commune, since it patently displeased the Soviets, did not prove too difficult, but the practical organization of these collective units offered no such easy escape. It was Ho Chi Minh himself who provided the solution when he announced that, "at the present time the state farm is the future image of the agricultural cooperative." [32] The use of the term "state farm" suggested that North Vietnamese agriculture was being developed along Soviet lines and was modeling itself upon Soviet state farms. However, he went on to say that the state farms would also operate processing plants for their agricultural products and would "supply industry [presumably home industry] as well as raw materials and products for fraternal countries." [33] Other press and radio pronouncements made it clear that the state farms were going to develop their own militias, would have an industrial function, and

[32] *Nhan Dan,* Oct. 5, 1960.
[33] *Ibid.*

would embody an unspecified degree of communal living, all of which are attributes peculiar to Chinese communes.

This typically Vietnamese ambiguity appears to have satisfied both the Soviet Union and China. The former would have found it difficult to object to a system of agricultural development which used current Soviet terms, while the latter could scarcely criticize something so closely resembling her own communes even if the name was not used. The example of agricultural collectivization has been chosen because it illustrates the kind of problem which DRV leaders were constantly encountering in so many spheres as a result of the differences between China and the Soviet Union. They found themselves driven to seeking solutions which were not always ideal for their own immediate internal problems but which were calculated to avoid causing offense to either China or the Soviet Union. Again, the establishment of state farms with some of the attributes of communes reveals the sort of deceit and ambiguity to which the Vietnamese had to resort. It must have been a humiliating experience for them but one they were obliged to undergo if they hoped to continue to maintain friendly relations with both Communist bloc leaders.

And there was no respite from these pin pricks. They were ever present in virtually every sphere of activity, and, however hard the Vietnamese might try to avoid offending their troublesome partners by passing over matters in discreet silence, either the Soviet Union or China would almost invariably call attention to anything it construed as supporting its own position. Peking Radio, for example, announced on November 2, 1960 that the fourth volume of Mao's works had been put on sale in

Hanoi on October 28 and went on to describe how large numbers of eager Vietnamese crowded the bookshops and quickly bought up the entire edition. Failure to offer this book for sale would have offended the Chinese, so the Vietnamese did place it in the bookshops, but they would have sought to avoid publicity for their action lest the Soviet Union take offense. Neither Hanoi Radio in its domestic or foreign broadcasts nor VNA made any mention of the book, but Peking delightedly seized upon the incident and tossed it into the area of the dispute. The North Vietnamese leaders could hardly be blamed if they conceived a heartfelt, if carefully concealed, dislike of both the Soviet Union and China for thus complicating their lives and increasing the difficulty of every problem.

THE 1960 MEETING OF 81 PARTIES IN MOSCOW

A fresh crisis in the Sino-Soviet dispute arose in November 1960 when the delegations from 81 Communist parties met at a congress in Moscow. In the course of this meeting it became apparent to all that the gulf dividing the two countries was too wide to be bridged. Moreover, the Soviets made no secret of their intention to force other Communist parties to make a choice between themselves and the Chinese. In the words of one commentator:

Some parties wanted to patch up a compromise "for fear that similar differences might arise in their own parties," but this would not do. It was impossible for the two views to be reconciled. A choice had to be made, a clear verdict given.[34]

[34] Article by Edward Crankshaw, *The Observer*, May 6, 1962.

The questions at issue and the discussion of them which took place are now too well known to require repeating here,[35] but the heat of the disputes and the obvious danger of a top-to-bottom split in the world Communist movement must have been profoundly disquieting to the DRV delegation led by Ho Chi Minh. It was no longer the moment for placatory verbal ambiguities, for judicious swaying from one side to another in order to preserve a balance that would produce maximum benefits for North Vietnam. If a schism were to divide communism, North Vietnam would be among the first of its victims. The danger was real and immediate, and there is every indication that Ho Chi Minh devoted all his efforts in Moscow to attempts at mediation.[36]

A drafting committee was set up and given the task of producing a final declaration that would satisfy both the Soviet Union and China. Because of the uncompromising Soviet attitude this must have been an undertaking of the utmost difficulty involving lengthy and embittered debate. The details of the committee's proceedings have — understandably — never been disclosed, but there is reason to believe that its final success was due in no small measure to the help it received from Ho Chi Minh, whose long experience and proven ability in the political arena must have been tested to the limit. The document that the drafting committee produced could have satisfied nobody completely, but it did offer

[35] See, for example, Donald S. Zagoria, *The Sino-Soviet Conflict, 1956–1961* (Princeton, N.J.: Princeton University Press, 1962); William E. Griffith, "The November 1960 Moscow Meeting: A Preliminary Reconstruction," *The China Quarterly*, July–Sept. 1962; Edward Crankshaw's articles in *The Observer*, Feb. 12, 19, 1961 and May 6, 20, 1962, etc.

[36] K. V. Narain in *The Hindu Weekly Review*, Feb. 6, 13, 1961.

an alternative to splitting the Communist world into two hostile factions; as such it was accepted by all the participating parties.

In the opinion of Zagoria the final declaration was

. . . not a real compromise of Soviet and Chinese views, but a collation of them. While the document, in its broad outlines, must be regarded as a Soviet "victory," its ambiguities and qualifications were so numerous that it could hardly serve as a guide for any of the Communist parties. Both the Soviet Union and China could and did derive different conclusions from it. The ostensible Soviet victory was thus bought at the very heavy price of an unworkable compromise which served clearly to demonstrate that the Soviets were no longer able unilaterally to dictate law for the entire international Communist movement.[37]

Zagoria's judgment was confirmed by the Belgian Communist Party Politburo, which stated that the final declaration was "so loaded . . . that it was possible to quote from it to support the statement, the defense, and the application of political views diametrically opposed and often outrageously divergent. . . ." [38]

If the immediate danger had been averted, this had been accomplished only at the cost of an unsatisfactory statement that permitted the two parties to the dispute to continue along their divergent courses, a solution which delayed the day of reckoning but which ensured that the reckoning would be infinitely more difficult and disastrous when it eventually arrived.

As far as North Vietnam was concerned the acceptance of the final declaration by the assembled representatives of 81 Communist parties in Moscow was a

[37] Zagoria, op. cit., pp. 367–368.
[38] Belgian Communist Party Politburo statement in Le Drapeau Rouge, Feb. 22, 1962 and cited by Griffith, op. cit., p. 55.

matter for uninhibited rejoicing. The danger of a split in the Communist movement had been removed, if only temporarily, and North Vietnam was still free to continue on her carefully charted course between the Soviet Union and China. An overwhelming feeling of relief is reflected in the almost hysterical reception of the news in Hanoi. From December 6 onward Hanoi Radio broadcast the whole statement, parts of the statement, comments on the statement, praise for the statement interminably, day after day, completely upsetting the normal schedule of broadcasting. Its daily programs read at dictation speed were lengthened and devoted exclusively to publicizing the statement so that the glad tidings should reach everybody as quickly as possible. Praise for the statement was fulsome and lavish in the extreme, and no adjective was considered too extravagant by the broadcasters and journalists. Since the contents of the final declaration alone could scarcely have provided anyone with cause for rejoicing, one is obliged to conclude that this hysteria in North Vietnam was occasioned by the feeling of having escaped disaster by a hairbreadth, a feeling which must have been shared by all the DRV leaders. No other explanation will account for the behavior of Hanoi Radio at that time.

The reactions of the ill-informed peasant or worker to the extraordinary outburst must remain a mystery. It should be remembered that no publication and no radio broadcast inside North Vietnam had yet so much as hinted that anything other than complete unanimity of view on all questions existed among governments and parties of the Communist bloc. In his book mentioned earlier M. Tongas[39] showed that the North Vietnamese

[39] Gérard Tongas, *J'ai vécu dans l'enfer communiste au Nord Vietnam et j'ai choisi la liberté* (Paris: Les Nouvelles Editions Debresse, 1961).

man in the street was not as aware of differences between Communists as might be imagined by outside observers, but the prevailing absence of factual news made
him susceptible to rumors. He must surely have sus-
pected that something of major import had taken place
in Moscow, but we have no information about the nature of the interpretations he may have put on it.

While all DRV newspapers carried daily articles praising the final statement and describing the unbridled joy
with which the news of it was received by the population, *Nhan Dan* published an important article commenting on the document and apparently reflecting the
considered views of the party.[40] The most striking feature
of the article is the similarity between its language and
that of a *People's Daily* article on the same subject which
was published in China on the same day. Although the
Moscow final declaration made no reference to China
as one of the two largest countries of the socialist camp
and did not mention the need for strengthening unity
and solidarity between the Soviet Union and China, the
North Vietnamese and Chinese articles did both of these
things. Both interpreted the declaration as an appeal for
increased struggle throughout the world, stressing its
"fighting aspects" and its call for "joint struggles." Such
similarities are too great to be attributed to pure coincidence and indicate joint discussions of the Moscow
declaration by Chinese and Vietnamese leaders. Possibly
this interpretation of the document was part of the price
demanded of Ho Chi Minh by the Chinese in return for
their agreement to accept it.

After appealing for "solidarity and unity of mind"
among the member states of the bloc and among their

[40] Editorial, *Nhan Dan*, Dec. 7, 1960.

Communist and workers' parties, the *Nhan Dan* editorial continued:

The Soviet Union is the mightiest country in the socialist camp and the CPSU is the most experienced vanguard party of the international Communist movement. At the same time, the Soviet Union and China are the two largest countries in the socialist bloc, and the CPSU and the CCP are the two largest and most responsible parties in the international Communist movement. For that reason particular importance should be attached to the strengthening of the solidarity and unity of mind between the Soviet Union and China.[41]

The fact that these two countries and their parties were singled out for special comment could indicate to North Vietnamese experienced in reading between the lines of the Communist press that all was not well, but whether or not it was understood in this fashion by the readers of *Nhan Dan*, it must be considered the first public reference in North Vietnam to the existence of important Sino-Soviet differences.

All DRV references to peaceful coexistence since the second half of 1959 have had to be couched in language implying that the war going on in South Vietnam is entirely justifiable, for, although the Vietnamese Communists may shrug their shoulders at the West and deny any responsibility for the fighting, such an attitude on their part would not be accepted for one moment by other Communist countries. It is therefore interesting to examine the *Nhan Dan* editorial in order to see how it disposed of this thorny question. The argument is somewhat tortuous and runs along the lines that peaceful coexistence and the development of indigenous revo-

[41] *Ibid.*

lutions in capitalist countries should be practiced simultaneously because "peaceful coexistence is a form of the class struggle between socialism and capitalism." In "colonial and dependent territories" the revolutionary struggle should take two forms, "peaceful and nonpeaceful," and all efforts must be directed toward "strengthening the united national front." Only after such an introduction does the editorial go on to imply that since the United States is building up an aggressive military base in South Vietnam the war there is entirely consistent with a policy of peace because it is being fought to "prevent the warlike imperialists from launching a world war. . . ." After this example of verbal sleight of hand *Nhan Dan* went on to argue that "all schemes of war preparation by imperialism should be resolutely smashed."

Some weeks later, when there had been time for the initial Hanoi hysteria to abate and the press and radio campaign to end, *Nhan Dan* published another editorial on the subject under the unwieldy title, "Under the Banner of the Moscow Statement and of the Resolution of our Party Congress, Let Us Unite and Endeavor to Lead Our People's Revolutionary Cause to Complete Victory." [42] On this occasion the polemics had been dropped, together with argumentation concerning peaceful coexistence, and the writer's attention was concentrated on the more important questions of political relationships within the bloc. For example:

We should close the ranks of the world's Communist parties around the CPSU, the most experienced contingent, which was the first to have carried high the victorious banner of proletarian revolution and has been marching in the van in the building of socialism and communism. We should un-

[42] *Ibid.*, Jan. 13, 1961.

ceasingly strengthen our solidarity with the CCP, which has recorded great successes in leading the 650 million Chinese people to carry out the national democratic revolution and to win great achievements in building socialism in one of the biggest countries in the world.[43]

It is apparent that after the stormy and anxious period of the Third Congress of the Lao Dong Party, with its short-lived swing toward the Soviet Union, and of the Moscow Congress of 81 parties North Vietnam had returned to the more familiar territory of the neutral ground between the two antagonists and was once again striving to maintain friendly relations with both. There was only one major difference. The Vietnamese Communist leadership had been badly frightened by the possibility of a schism in the world Communist movement and was more aware than ever of the overriding need to preserve some form of unity between Moscow and Peking.

CRISIS IN LAOS

Fighting in the curious three-sided Laotian war that had dragged on in desultory fashion over a long period reached a critical stage during the early months of 1961. Laotian politics are extremely involved and on occasion baffle even specialists in Laotian affairs. Fortunately it is not necessary to describe the happenings there but simply to state that the war was of particular interest to North Vietnam, the Soviet Union, and China for different reasons. The Soviet Union, as Co-Chairman of the 1954 Geneva Conference on Indochina which established independent Laos, carries a special responsibility shared

[43] *Ibid.*

with the United Kingdom for developments in that country. China was affected by the fact that she has a common frontier with Laos and that the fighting there had led to the introduction of United States troops into the territory. It is also possible that China regards Laos as falling within her own sphere of special influence and for that reason seeks to exercise some measure of control over the country's affairs, but this theory need not be discussed here. The North Vietnam regime founded the pro-Communist Pathet Lao organization in Laos, trained, armed, and developed it, and provided North Vietnamese troops to assist its military operations. Prince Souphanouvong, the nominal leader of the Pathet Lao, is married to a Vietnamese who has for years been an important member of the Lao Dong Party, and he has himself spent more time in Vietnam than in his native Laos. Moreover, since the principal route for the supply of men and arms to the Communist insurgents fighting in South Vietnam lies through eastern Laos, North Vietnam is committed to the defense of at least that part of the Laotian territory.

Prince Norodom Sihanouk of Cambodia suggested, as is his wont when conflicts occur in any part of the world, that the Laotian situation might be resolved by an international conference in Geneva, and this was the starting point for a complex series of differences among the Soviet Union, China, and North Vietnam. Khrushchev wrote a letter to Sihanouk on January 7, 1961 [44] in which he expressed his support for the suggested international conference. North Vietnam, which had for some time been advocating in its press the return of the International Control Commission (ICC) to Laos and

[44] It was summarized by TASS on Jan. 12, 1961.

the convening of the international conference,[45] supported the Soviet attitude. China, however, had adopted
a different position. Chen Yi, it is true, had made the
suggestion in a letter he wrote on December 28, 1960
that the ICC return to Laos, but the conditions which
he imposed governing its return were sufficient to ensure
that this would be impossible. China did not support the
holding of a conference but rather, in newspaper articles
and broadcasts, advocated a continuation of the Laotian
popular struggle. Indeed, a *People's Daily* article on the
resolutions of the Afro-Asian Solidarity Committee Conference pointedly omitted the resolution that advocated
a return of the ICC to Laos and the convening of a
conference.[46]

The pattern of alignments was changed when the
King of Laos made a declaration of Laotian neutrality
on February 19, 1961 and was promptly assailed by adverse comments from the Pathet Lao, China, and North
Vietnam. The Soviet Union ignored the declaration and
refrained from making any comment. In the course of
an interview broadcast by Moscow Radio on March 22,
1961 the Laotian leader Prince Souvanna Phouma proposed that a cease-fire in Laos should precede the meeting of an international conference. On the following day
VNA issued a bulletin stating that Souvanna Phouma
had made this suggestion at a "recent news conference
in New Delhi," while a *People's Daily* article urged the
Laotians to "step up their struggle and further develop
the great victory recently achieved." The tone of this

[45] See, for example, the article on this subject published in *Nhan
Dan*, Jan. 6, 1961, which stated that "the requisite conditions are
now ripe" for the return of the Commission and the holding of a
conference.

[46] Editorial, *People's Daily*, Jan. 26, 1961.

article made it clear that China was opposed to a cease-fire as a precondition of a conference.

As the wrangle over a cease-fire and an international conference continued, the Soviet Union broadcast a single program in the Vietnamese language which had all the appearance of a direct appeal to North Vietnam, for it was not repeated in any other language. The fact that it was directed to North Vietnam is strongly indicative of Soviet belief that it was the North Vietnamese who controlled the fighting in Laos and who in the last resort would decide whether or not to call a cease-fire. Arguing that the Soviet Union did not demand a cease-fire as a "precondition" and that the international conference on Laos was the "main point" of the Soviet plan, the Soviet radio broadcast then stated that nevertheless "a cease-fire in Laos will help to create a favorable atmosphere for negotiations." [47]

Ho Chi Minh was well placed for equivocation about matters concerning Laos because he controlled three radio stations, the Voice of Vietnam, the clandestine Voice of the Laotian Kingdom, and the Pathet Lao Radio, all of which appear to be transmitted from the same place in North Vietnam. Ho is a past master in operations of this kind and contrived to create an impression of DRV moderation and Laotian impatience by attacking the suggestion of a prior cease-fire in broadcasts from the Laotian stations while maintaining a more restrained tone in DRV broadcasts. Answering the Soviet appeal, the Pathet Lao Radio demanded that a cease-fire be concluded "simultaneously" with the convocation of the international conference and adopted a belligerent tone toward the United States and Thailand. If the

[47] Soviet broadcast in Vietnamese, Apr. 4, 1961.

United States and Thai "aggressors" really wanted a cease-fire, it said, then all they had to do was to stop their attacks against the "legal government" of Laos and withdraw United States, Thai, and Nationalist Chinese personnel, together with their arms, from Laos.[48] A cease-fire was eventually implemented, and the international conference convened. The incident is noteworthy, however, because it demonstrates that North Vietnam is prepared to resist Soviet pressures and to disagree publicly with declared Soviet policies in matters which directly affect her own internal situation — provided she is certain of Chinese backing.

ALTERED BALANCE OF THE LEADERSHIP

An important change in the power balance within the DRV leadership took place in the spring of 1961 when Nguyen Chi Thanh, head of the Vietnamese People's Army Political Department and a member of the Politburo, was stripped of his military rank and transferred to other duties. In September 1959 Thanh had been promoted to the highest grade of general, a rank hitherto held only by Vo Nguyen Giap, and his elevation had been an obvious move to reduce the importance of Giap. A close political ally of Truong Chinh, Thanh had long been identified with a pro-Chinese faction in the DRV leadership, but the reasons underlying his replacement cannot be defined accurately because of the scant information. Undoubtedly, since intense rivalry existed between Giap and Thanh, the personal element was involved, but it is still impossible to know whether or not

[48] Pathet Lao Radio, Apr. 6, 1961.

the move was brought about because of the Sino-Soviet dispute.

From early March 1961 the DRV press referred to Thanh as "Rural Affairs Chairman of the Party Central Committee" and ceased to employ his military title. As is usual in Communist states, the shift was foreshadowed by a change in ideological argumentation. During 1958 and 1959 DRV propaganda had regularly attacked the "pure militarists" in the army, by which they meant Vo Nguyen Giap. The impending move was presaged in an extremely tortuous article published in *Hoc Tap*.[49] Its author, General Hoang Van Thai, revealed that a major shift of power had taken place by demanding modernization and a "mastery of techniques" in the Vietnamese People's Army. Of course this was very dangerous ground in view of the conflicting attitudes of the Soviet Union and China, which explains why the article was filled with double-talk and ambiguities. The statement "Either we shall progress to acquire new techniques or we shall be exterminated" was balanced by lip service to the "decisive role of man," but the concluding portion of the article asserted, "The fact that we stress the decisive role of man in war does not mean that we deny the important role of techniques and weapons," a clear indication that a shift of power had taken place and that Giap — in ideological terms he is represented as the advocate of "techniques and weapons" — had struggled back to the top once more. A few weeks later Nguyen Chi Thanh was dismissed, and Giap was once more in control of the Vietnamese People's Army.

It is worth pausing at this juncture to consider the role of the Vietnamese People's Army. This large well-

[49] *Hoc Tap*, Dec. 1960.

trained military force is unquestionably the most powerful army in Southeast Asia. At the present time it carries
out a variety of tasks ranging from ensuring internal
security and safeguarding the Communist regime to supporting the Vietcong insurgents in South Vietnam and
the Pathet Lao in Laos, but its most important function
is, and must remain, the defense of North Vietnam
against external aggression. A glance at North Vietnam's
neighbors will suffice to show that the military strength
of Laos and Cambodia is slight and that neither country
could ever hope to challenge the military might of the
Vietnamese People's Army. South Vietnam commands
more powerful forces, but these are far from strong
enough to pose unaided a serious threat to North Vietnam. Conceivably, under certain circumstances the South
Vietnamese army reinforced by a Western army might
attack North Vietnam, but if this were ever to happen,
China would almost certainly come to North Vietnam's
defense — if only to safeguard her own frontiers. Therefore, if Laos, Cambodia, and South Vietnam are elimi-
nated as potential aggressors (Thailand might be added
to this number because her army is also too weak to
offer a real threat to the Vietnamese People's Army)
then only one country remains — China. It was pointed
out in an earlier chapter that the traditional Vietnamese
fears of Chinese expansion remain strong, and there are
excellent grounds for the belief that the principal *raison
d'être* of such a powerful army in North Vietnam today
is to protect North Vietnam against possible Chinese
aggression.

   Under circumstances such as these it would be folly
indeed for Ho Chi Minh to entrust the command of the
Vietnamese People's Army to anyone other than an

avowed enemy of China. More than any other Vietnamese leader, Giap is just such a person. It may well be that Ho Chi Minh's apprehension over the growing authority within the army of the pro-Chinese Nguyen Chi Thanh, and the danger this represented for the defense of North Vietnamese territory, are the real reasons why Giap was restored to full and undisputed control of the Vietnamese People's Army in March 1961. If this line of argument is carried a little further, it suggests that a set of detailed plans for the defense of North Vietnam against attack by China must lie ready in the DRV Ministry of Defense at Hanoi. Moreover, in order to be effective these plans would have to be kept constantly up to date, changing from time to time so as to take account of new developments in China's military strength; and that implies the necessity for North Vietnam to keep herself well informed of all military developments in China, even those of a secret nature. She can obtain the necessary information only by means of espionage. It would therefore be surprising if North Vietnam does not now have spies actively engaged in the collection of military intelligence inside the territory of her ally China.

ECONOMIC SETBACKS

Throughout the year 1960 North Vietnam suffered serious setbacks in every branch of the national economy and attributed the lion's share of the blame to "poor agricultural production . . . as well as weak points and shortcomings in economic controls." [50] In mid-1960 plan targets were reduced and norms adjusted downward so as to avoid disclosing the full extent of the failure to

[50] Communiqué of the DRV Council of Ministers, Aug. 4, 1961.

reach plan targets for the year. In 1961 it was again announced that

> In the present practical situation regarding the carrying out of the state plan in the last six months of the year, and in order to avoid unnecessary tensions in the improvement of the economy and the living standard of the people, the Council of Ministers has approved the proposals of the State Planning Committee and the Finance Ministry regarding the sound and effective adjustment in the norms of the state plan and the state budget for the last six months of the year.[51]

In plain English this meant that the targets accepted as reasonable at the beginning of the year were proving to be unattainable and so were being lowered.

Economic failure on a scale large enough to necessitate the lowering of plan targets in two consecutive years must have convinced the DRV leaders of the vulnerable situation of North Vietnam and of the pressing need for continued and increased economic aid from abroad. Yet the principal sources of such aid — the Soviet Union and the European satellites on the one hand and China on the other — were engaged in a bitter dispute, the consequences of which were unforeseeable. As North Vietnam's economic needs increased, the intensity of the dispute heightened, and with it the danger of losing a large part of the vital foreign aid.

There is much evidence to show that the North Vietnamese had fallen victims to Communist propaganda concerning the efficacy of aid and had expected far more than they received. Their disappointment was noticeable in their relationships with the visiting bloc technicians and aid administrators. M. Tongas cites many such in-

[51] *Ibid.*

stances which he witnessed.[52] In April 1959 Ho Chi Minh found it necessary to remonstrate with his compatriots and to tell them that they simply had to learn to cooperate with the foreign technicians. Continuing economic failures exacerbated the situation, and relations deteriorated further until Truong Chinh made a speech on the subject which received wide circulation in the DRV press. He alleged that certain cadres and party members

. . . lack modesty in their dealings with technicians from brother countries and do not try to learn from them. They do not try to apply creatively the experiences of brother countries to the conditions of our country. They are not friendly toward these technicians and do not respect them. They do not try to create favorable conditions to facilitate the work of these comrade technicians.[53]

Agricultural collectivization was still proving to be the greatest disappointment of all, and its failure obliged even as highly placed a leader as Le Duan, First Secretary of the Lao Dong Party, to eat his words publicly. In his report to the Third Party Congress in September 1960 he said

. . . we must, of necessity, educate and imbue them [the peasants] with socialist ideology; at the same time we must devise appropriate measures to sever their economic ties with the bourgeoisie and to restrict and eliminate their spontaneous tendency toward capitalism.[54]

Less than a year later he was writing

The tendency to restrict the productive activities and private undertakings of the families of cooperative members — a

[52] Tongas, *op. cit.*

[53] Truong Chinh, speech to the Party Central Re-education Conference, Mar. 13, 1961.

[54] VNA, Sept. 11, 1960.

tendency originating from the fear that cooperative members will enrich themselves in the "capitalist" way — even when these activities and undertakings are not harmful to the cooperative production is obviously unsuitable to the new situation in rural areas.[55]

The disastrous decline in agricultural production was indeed rapid, and Le Duan showed that he proposed loosening controls still further in order to improve the situation. In the same article he stated that private operations (i.e., farming private plots of land) in 1961 were providing cooperative members with some 30 to 40 per cent of their total income even though private plots comprised only 5 per cent of the total area of the cooperatives. In 1962, he forecast, private operations would provide cooperative members with about 55 per cent of their income. However, Le Duan still regarded the agricultural situation of North Vietnam as closer to that of China than the Soviet Union and implied that the Chinese-style agricultural organization was the only one suited to North Vietnam. In the Soviet Union and European bloc countries, he said, collectivization was accompanied by mechanization, but in China, North Korea, and North Vietnam a "new situation" existed because collectivization had been carried out without modern farming equipment. These countries have been able to "create a new productive force simply by regrouping the means of production and by reorganizing labor." [56]

The war in South Vietnam was a further source of disquiet, for the DRV committal of greater forces in the South had resulted only in increased American deter-

[55] Article by Le Duan, *Hoc Tap*, Aug. 1961.
[56] Le Duan's speech to the Party Conference on Agricultural Goals, published in *Nhan Dan*, Oct. 3, 1961.

mination to defend the government of President Ngo
Dinh Diem. More and more United States troops were
sent to South Vietnam, and their participation in the
fighting was steadily becoming more direct. Prospects of
a quick military victory there, and access to South Vietnam's rice surplus had vanished. Instead of providing a
solution to North Vietnam's economic problems the
adventure in South Vietnam was proving an ever-growing drain on resources and was inspiring Communist
criticisms of Ho Chi Minh for causing a build-up of
United States military strength in Southeast Asia.

The worsening economic situation, the inefficacy of
aid from abroad, and personal antagonisms between the
North Vietnamese people and the foreign technicians
who had come to educate and help them surely worried
Ho Chi Minh and his colleagues. Even if untroubled
unity existed within the whole Communist bloc, the
situation of North Vietnam would give cause for some
alarm, but unity had long since been shattered, and both
China and the Soviet Union had showed every sign of
persisting in their quarrel regardless of its consequences
for other Communist countries, some of whom had
shown themselves ready both to take sides in the dispute
and to take part in the mutual recriminations. North
Vietnam could afford no such indulgence because she
badly needed all the economic assistance she could obtain from every quarter. To antagonize any Communist
country would be tantamount to inviting that country
to cease supplying aid, and the serious economic failures
in North Vietnam simply would not permit this. Consequently, Ho Chi Minh found himself in mid-1961
more heavily committed than ever before to his policy
of remaining on good terms with all Communist coun-

tries, of avoiding any participation in the Sino-Soviet dispute, and of using any means at his disposal to bring this dangerous conflict to an end.

THE TWENTY-SECOND CPSU CONGRESS AND AFTER

October 1961 was from beginning to end a month of unpleasant shocks for all Communists, with the removal of Stalin from the Kremlin mausoleum, the attacks on Albania at the Twenty-Second CPSU Congress, and Chou En-lai's walkout from the Congress. Even early in the month the signs were ominous, for Khrushchev's attack on the Albanian leadership was published in Tirana and a counterattack launched. Fuel was added to the flames when a Chinese delegate to a Congress of Albanian Women praised the "correct leadership of the Albanian Workers' Party headed by its long tested leader, Enver Hoxha." It was no surprise when Ho Chi Minh decided to lead the North Vietnamese delegation to Moscow in person and interrupted his journey in Peking to confer with Mao Tse-tung and other Chinese leaders. The proceedings of the Congress are too well known to require further description. Khrushchev unleashed new attacks on Albania, and Chou En-lai walked out in the middle of the proceedings after appealing for an end to open polemics and laying flowers on the grave of Stalin. Of the 66 speakers at the Congress, only 22 avoided reference to Albania, among whom were numbered the North Vietnamese.

Ho Chi Minh was in a most difficult predicament because whatever his actions, they were likely to be misconstrued by the leading antagonists. To have walked out of the Congress with Chou En-lai would have caused serious offense to the Soviet Union, while his continuing presence there might prove equally offensive to the Chinese. Ho escaped from his dilemma in the most diplomatic way open to him by proceeding on a tour of the Soviet Union. His attitude toward the whole business was summed up in a cable that the DRV National Assembly dispatched to the Congress, pledging the Vietnamese people to struggle in order to strengthen the unity and uniformity of mind inside the socialist camp — a praiseworthy ideal but one which events of the Congress rendered a shade impractical. No matter how hard one tried to avoid the subjects in dispute, there was always a danger that one might commit oneself unwittingly, and this seems to have happened to the ultracautious Ho Chi Minh during a Moscow Radio interview on November 6 which was broadcast to Vietnam. His reference to the "12 states" of the socialist camp was excised from the version of the interview broadcast on the Soviet Home Service although the rebroadcast was postponed until November 10, the day after Ho concluded his final meeting with Khrushchev. He left Moscow the following day and spent four days in Peking conferring with Chinese leaders; the subjects of these discussions have never been disclosed.

DRV reaction to the happenings at the Twenty-Second Congress was circumspect in the extreme. Reports on the proceedings were publicized by both press and radio — not to have done so would surely have aroused suspicions in the minds of the North Vietnamese people that all was not well — but the references to Albania were omitted. Although the meeting was hailed as a brilliant success, as Communist meetings invariably are, and Congress documents were published in *Nhan Dan* from November 4 on, none of the individual decisions was accorded DRV approval with the exception of the CPSU Program — called the "Communist Manifesto of Our Era." A hint of discord was perceptible in the speech made by Nguyen Duy Trinh on the anniversary of the October Revolution in which he described the "ideological unanimity of all parties" as basic and argued that "we" should resolve "contradictions" and "try our best to avoid losses to international solidarity." [57] From all the DRV comment made about the Twenty-Second Congress of the CPSU, the two features most clearly discernible were embarrassment and apprehension.

The anniversary of the Albanian Party of Labor falls on November 8, and in 1961 it coincided with one of the highest peaks of the Sino-Soviet dispute to date. Among the Communist bloc parties only three sent telegrams of greeting to the Albanian party that year — the Chinese and North Korean parties and the Lao Dong Party. The CCP voiced full support for Albania and exploited the occasion to engage in indirect attacks on the Soviet Union, while the North Korean party dispatched a correctly formal message of greetings to the Central Committee of the Albanian Party of Labor and thereafter ignored the anniversary. The DRV telegram was careful not to express any opinion about the correctness or otherwise of the Albanian leadership, but North Vietnam marked the occasion with copious and fulsome praise for the Albanian party. The first impression created by this flood of approbation was that North Vietnam had decided to align herself with China on the Albanian question, but closer study revealed that great care had

[57] VNA, Nov. 8, 1961.

gone into the wording of every statement made. The Albanian party was so highly praised that approval of the leadership might seem to be implied, but no approval was stated. Indeed, no judgment at all of the Albanian First Secretary Enver Hoxha and his colleagues was made.

By this uneasy compromise solution Ho Chi Minh indicated unmistakably to the Soviets that he disapproved of their attacks on Albania and that North Vietnam would continue to regard Albania as a full member of the socialist bloc whatever the Soviet Union might think. On the other hand, by his failure to endorse Hoxha's leadership or to express any opinion concerning its correctness he left China in no doubt about his disapproval of her wholehearted espousal of the Albanian cause. This attitude was obviously the outcome of careful consideration of the dispute by the DRV leadership, and it is one from which North Vietnam has not deviated since that time. Since no responsible Communist could approve, in theory at least, of a quarrel which endangered bloc unity, the conciliatory attitude of the North Vietnamese leaders would be difficult to attack. In fact neither the Soviet Union nor China has attacked her stand over Albania although it is one hardly calculated to afford much comfort to either of these countries.

INCREASED CHINESE PRESSURES

By exploiting to the full the military situation in South Vietnam, where United States aid to the South Vietnamese authorities continued to increase steadily and to enable the South Vietnamese forces to inflict some heavy defeats upon the insurgents, China attempted to establish closer ties with North Vietnam, with the apparent intention of winning Vietnamese support in her dispute with the Soviet Union. When replying to a note of October 30 which North Vietnam had sent to 103 governments complaining about United States aggression in South Vietnam, China stated that the CPR government and people "cannot remain indifferent" to United States action in South Vietnam.[58] Only a few days after this Chinese reply the United States State Department published a "White Paper" containing much documentary proof of DRV participation in the war being waged in South Vietnam, an act greeted with volumes of abuse in North Vietnam and one which was described by a spokesman of the DRV Foreign Ministry as "preparing the way for United States intervention" in North Vietnam. On December 7 and 8, respectively, NCNA and VNA announced that a Chinese military delegation would visit North Vietnam.

The different reasons given by the two countries for the visit indicate that the arrangements had been made hurriedly and suggest that the Vietnamese were not entirely happy about this new Chinese initiative. VNA asserted that the Chinese delegation would visit North Vietnam to celebrate the seventeenth anniversary of the Vietnamese People's Army (the anniversary falls on December 22), while NCNA described it as a "friendly visit." In a newspaper article about the visit General Le Quang Dao wrote the customary clichés about its "significance" for strengthening "the long-standing friendship between the peoples and armies of Vietnam and China" — astonishingly, in spite of all the historical evi-

[58] CPR note to the DRV government, Nov. 29, 1961.

dence of its inaccuracy, this statement is repeatedly made by DRV leaders — but carefully avoided any reference to cooperation in the military field between the two countries.[59] The importance of the visit was heightened by the rupture of diplomatic relations between the Soviet Union and Albania on December 10 and by the VNA publication of a factual report on the Albanian-Soviet notes on the day preceding the arrival of the Chinese in Hanoi.

Immediately prior to the Chinese visit to North Vietnam an important difference of opinion had arisen between Peking and Moscow over the theme of the Stockholm meeting of the World Peace Council (WPC) scheduled to take place on December 16. While the Soviet Union wished the WPC to sponsor a 1962 Congress devoted solely to the subject of disarmament, China demanded that the subject of this Congress should be imperialism and the national liberation struggle. Support for the Chinese suggestion was not large, comprising Albania, North Korea, some Latin American parties, and North Vietnam, and it could well have been the DRV backing on this question which suggested to the Chinese that the North Vietnamese were not entirely free agents in matters concerning liberation struggles but were bound by their own circumstances to proclaim support for them. Having justified the South Vietnamese war by describing it as a national liberation struggle, and being irrevocably committed to continuing the fighting there, North Vietnam could scarcely avoid backing any Communist action designed to encourage the waging of national liberation struggles.

The Chinese military delegation, under the leadership

[59] Article by Le Quang Dao in *Nhan Dan*, Dec. 14, 1961.

of Marshal Yeh Chien-ying, arrived in Hanoi on December 15, and the visit was accorded maximum publicity by both North Vietnam and China. The Soviet Union, however, evinced her own displeasure at the turn of events by failing to mention either the Chinese visit or the anniversary of the Vietnamese People's Army. To what extent the delegation was forced upon North Vietnam by Chinese insistence is uncertain, but it is quite plain that at least some of the Vietnamese leaders were not overjoyed at the presence of the Chinese soldiers. Vo Nguyen Giap, for instance, who made the principal speech at a banquet for the visitors on the evening of December 15 in his capacity as Minister of Defense and Commander-in-Chief of the Vietnamese People's Army, barely remained within the bounds of politeness. He certainly made flattering references to the Chinese People's Army, but whenever he did so he was careful to counterbalance them with still more flattering references to the Soviet Red Army. After referring to the Chinese army as a source of "valuable experience" for the Vietnamese People's Army, he went on to praise the Soviet Union's "advanced military science," and he continued in this fashion throughout the entire speech. His oration is a model of studied rudeness conveyed through courteous and sometimes flattering words.

The purpose behind the Chinese visit was revealed in a message of greeting sent by Lin Piao to Vo Nguyen Giap for the Vietnamese People's Army anniversary, which raised the question of mutual defense agreements between China and North Vietnam. The text included the passage, "We . . . will make joint efforts with you to defend the security of our respective countries," [60]

[60] NCNA, Dec. 21, 1961.

and the proposal was repeated, though in less precise terms, in a speech made by General Lo Jui-ching at Peking when he spoke of "joint efforts" by the peoples of China and Vietnam. However, when the DRV press and radio accorded Lin Piao's message only scant mention, China appeared to take the hint and did not repeat his proposal. It is interesting to note some of the deletions made by VNA from its reports of speeches, Vietnamese as well as Chinese, during the visit of the military delegation. Vo Nguyen Giap's thanks to the Chinese people and government, which he expressed in his impolite banquet speech, for their "sympathy and support" in the struggle to reunite Vietnam were omitted from the VNA version but included in the NCNA report. Other omissions from VNA reports were Yeh Chien-ying's thanks for DRV support in the "struggle against United States imperialist aggression," General Liu Ya-lou's call for unity between the Chinese and Vietnamese armies, Yeh Chien-ying's remark that socialist states "cooperate closely . . . in the common struggle," praise for the "military ideas of Mao Tse-tung" voiced by the Vietnamese director of an artillery school visited by the delegation, and so on. The censorship indicated clearly the coolness with which the DRV leaders greeted the new Chinese initiative.

Even though North Vietnam was unenthusiastic, the Chinese proposals found a sympathetic audience among the hard-pressed guerrillas fighting in South Vietnam. The National Front for the Liberation of South Vietnam (NFLSV), which had been established by Hanoi a year earlier, took the unprecedented step of differing from its Northern masters in a note which it sent to foreign governments on December 22, 1961, the day after Lin Piao dispatched his message. After declaring the South Vietnamese people's determination to fight on to the end, the Front said that "if the need should arise," it would appeal to friendly countries for help, "including material aid." A similar threat was later to be made by the South Vietnamese People's Revolutionary Party (PRP), a Communist party formed in South Vietnam in January 1962, which immediately incorporated itself into the NFLSV and claimed for itself the "vanguard role" in the Front. In a statement issued by its Central Committee the PRP threatened that it would, "if necessary . . . call on the DRV government . . . for aid in materials and men." [61] The two warnings from South Vietnam reflected an obvious dissatisfaction with the progress of the war there, and probably with the assistance being sent clandestinely by North Vietnam, and revealed a division of thinking among Vietnamese Communists which might well give rise to serious consequences if the rift between the Soviet Union and China widens further. Although the Chinese may have misjudged the mood of the Communist leadership in North Vietnam, their appreciation of Communist feelings in South Vietnam was accurate.

The failure of the high-ranking Chinese military delegation to win any DRV acceptance for the idea of a defensive military treaty or for any form of military cooperation between the two countries served to make the position adopted by North Vietnam perfectly plain to the two largest Communist states. At the end of 1961 North Vietnam had shown by its failure to report any of the attacks made on Albania at the Twenty-Second Congress of the CPSU and by its continuing treatment of

[61] Statement broadcast by Hanoi Radio, Apr. 24, 1962.

Albania as a full member of the socialist bloc that it could not be forced to accede to Soviet demands even though its need for Soviet aid was desperate. Equally, its unyielding resistance to Chinese blandishments and pressures made it clear that North Vietnam refused to be intimidated by the great size and geographical proximity of China into accepting Chinese political or military direction. Its stand remained unaltered. It disapproved of the dispute and would ally itself completely with neither party to it. It would work for its settlement and for the establishment of a new unity of mind within the socialist bloc. Conflicting opinions might have been expressed by Communists fighting in South Vietnam, but no dissenting voices were heard in North Vietnam, where Ho Chi Minh remained undisputed master and imposed his own unity upon his subordinates.

THE WAR IN SOUTH VIETNAM

The growing necessity for North Vietnam to acquire by one means or another some of South Vietnam's rice surplus was underlined by the customary reviews of progress during the past year made at the beginning of 1962. The extent of North Vietnam's failure to overcome the shortage of food is vividly illustrated by a comparison of figures provided by Nguyen Duy Trinh, Chairman of the State Planning Commission. In his report to the National Assembly on April 14, 1961 he announced that rice production during the year would amount to 5.5 million tons, but when he reported on production achievements for the year on January 7, 1962 he stated, "We have harvested 4.6 million tons of rice," and there is reason to believe even this figure was exaggerated. At about the same time a despondent newspaper article declared categorically that North Vietnam would never be able to produce sufficient rice to feed the constantly increasing population and counseled people to accustom themselves to doing without rice and to live on other foods.[62] More and more attention was paid to the possibility of moving people from the overcrowded lowlands into the mountainous areas in an attempt to exploit these undeveloped regions, and in March an important decision to move industry and people into the highlands was made public.[63] Since then there has been a steady volume of reports on the difficulties encountered by this plan — hostility on the part of the highland dwellers (backward tribal peoples of non-Vietnamese race), sabotage of Vietnamese undertakings, difficulties of climate, health hazards, and much else besides. The scheme is obviously unpopular with both Vietnamese and highlanders, and the rapid pace at which it is being pushed forward is almost a guarantee of failure. Meanwhile, workers were leaving agricultural collectives in ever greater numbers to reap higher profits for less effort in the spreading black market that was thriving on food shortages and further aggravating an already difficult situation.[64]

United States help to the South Vietnamese authorities greatly exceeded the expectations of the DRV leaders, and the Communist insurgents in the South

[62] *Nhan Dan*, Jan. 8, 1962.
[63] VNA, Mar. 19, 1962.
[64] The newspaper *Thoi Moi* of Aug. 27, 1962 wrote:
In 1960 the turnover of the free markets [in Hanoi] was 12 million dongs. It has risen to 105 million dongs per annum in less than two years. Profits have grown to more than 40 per cent. Like a magnet, the free markets [of Hanoi] have attracted as many as 6,000 persons who have given up their old professions for trade.

were making little progress toward the attainment of their objectives. The establishment of a United States military command in South Vietnam was described as a threat to the security of North Vietnam, and on February 18, 1962 the government issued a pressing appeal for the "urgent study" of the situation in South Vietnam. China, following up her initiative at the end of 1961, issued a Foreign Ministry statement on February 24 which alleged that "United States aggression [in South Vietnam] constitutes a direct threat to the security of North Vietnam [and] seriously affects the security of China and the peace of Asia." [65] Soviet reaction was more cautious, and no Soviet action at all was taken until after the dispatch of a note by the DRV Foreign Minister, Ung Van Khiem, to the Co-Chairmen of the 1954 Geneva Conference, Britain and the Soviet Union, on March 15, 1962. The Soviet Foreign Ministry then issued a statement expressing support for North Vietnam's appeal of February 18 and sent copies to the governments of countries which participated in the Geneva Conference; but it ignored Ung Van Khiem's note of March 15, which urged the reconvening of the Geneva Conference. Evidently the Soviet Union was embarrassed by developments in South Vietnam while China was prepared to exploit them in order to court North Vietnam's favor.

Further differences between the Soviet Union and China became apparent when Nguyen Van Vinh addressed the North Vietnam National Assembly on April 18, 1962 and called for a reconvening of the Geneva Conference. Chinese press and radio reported his speech in detail, but the Soviets merely mentioned in one news-

[65] NCNA, Feb. 24, 1962.

paper that "a report on the South Vietnamese situation" was delivered to the National Assembly.[66] Both NCNA and Peking domestic broadcasts publicized the statement by the PRP in South Vietnam that this party would if necessary call on the North Vietnam government for aid in materiel and men,[67] but the Soviet Union failed to mention it at all. The Soviet Union has shown no enthusiasm for the PRP since its inception and has made very few references to it. None of the Soviet statements has ever admitted that this is a genuine Marxist-Leninist party.

A bombshell was exploded in mid-May 1962 when the International Control Commission reported to the Co-Chairmen of the Geneva Conference that North Vietnam had contravened the 1954 Geneva agreements by her participation in the South Vietnamese war. Since the Polish element of the ICC has always kept North Vietnam well informed about current Commission business, North Vietnam was aware that the report was in preparation and exerted every effort to prevent it; but the best it could manage was to persuade the Polish element to dissociate itself from the findings and to issue its own minority report, which did little to minimize the effects of the document.[68]

The North Vietnamese authorities, fully aware of the danger to their position if it was universally accepted that they were participating directly in the South Vietnamese war, issued frenzied denunciations and denials. North Vietnam attacked the ICC report, the ICC itself, the legality of its action, and so on. From mid-May on-

[66] *Izvestiya*, Apr. 19, 1962.
[67] First broadcast by Hanoi Radio on Apr. 24, 1962.
[68] Published by the British government as a White Paper (Cmnd. 1755) (London: H.M. Stationery Office, June 1962).

ward radio broadcasts and newspapers could speak of little else, while mass meetings were organized throughout the whole of North Vietnam and millions of signatures appeared on petitions of protest. It was against the Indian Chairman of the ICC, G. Parthasarathi, that the main weight of the attack was directed, for he not only bore the principal responsibility for the report but had appended a final statement rejecting the Polish minority report. Every crime in the Communist book was attributed to India in general and Mr. Parthasarathi in particular until observers wondered where it would all end.

After a few days initial delay, during which she restricted herself to echoing North Vietnamese attacks, China joined in the abuse on her own account on May 25, 1962, and her vilifications rivaled those of North Vietnam. The situation suited the Chinese perfectly because the state of Sino-Indian relations was already very bad as a result of the border dispute, and there was no reason at all why she should refrain from attacking the Indians. China was thus enabled to extract the maximum benefit from a situation in which her only expenditure was words.

The Soviet Union, on the other hand, found herself at a very grave disadvantage for the simple reason that she could not afford to attack India or even one of India's official representatives. Soviet failure to participate in the campaign of abuse undoubtedly angered North Vietnam, which was momentarily too enraged to appreciate the delicacy of the Soviet position. The North Vietnamese government issued an official declaration about the ICC report which, among other matters, alleged that the Canadian and Indian elements of the ICC had them-

selves violated the 1954 agreements and urged the Co-
Chairmen — of whom the Soviet Union was one — to
reject the report. The declaration was accorded the Chinese people's "full support" [69] and was followed by a
Chinese Foreign Ministry statement on June 9, 1962.
Acutely embarrassed by this turn of events, the Soviet
Union reported the DRV declaration in *Pravda* and in
TASS bulletins but made no comment at all. Vietnamese
annoyance is to be seen in the failure of North Vietnam
to send observers to the June conference of the Council
for Mutual Economic Assistance (CMEA) in Moscow.

Agreements signed at Geneva in July ended the war
in Laos and established her as a "neutral" country, which
required the withdrawal of all foreign troops and her
abandonment of SEATO protection. This solution appears to have pleased the Communist bloc as a whole
— and there were good reasons for their satisfaction, for
subsequent developments have showed that the agreement was a serious mistake on the part of the Western
powers — but there is evidence of disagreement in the
statements made about the reasons for the success of the
international conference. While the Soviet Union regarded the settlement as proof of the efficacy of peaceful
solutions, China maintained that agreement "was by no
means won easily" and stated that the struggle "was not
confined to the conference hall." [70] North Vietnam had
by then overcome its rage and regained its earlier position
in the center. Interviewed in Hanoi by correspondents
of *Izvestiya* and *Komsomolskaya Pravda*, Ho Chi Minh
opined that the Laotian settlement signified "that in
Southeast Asia, as in other places, all problems can be

[69] *People's Daily,* June 7, 1962.
[70] *Ibid.,* July 24, 1962.

solved satisfactorily by peaceful negotiations. . . ."[71]
Foreign Minister Ung Van Khiem said that the Laotian
agreement "proves the correctness and certain victory of
the peaceful foreign policy of the Soviet Union . . .
which undertakes to solve international disputes by negotiation," but took care to add, "This success has resulted
from the resolute and united struggle . . . against
United States armed interference."[72] In an obvious
reference to South Vietnam, *Nhan Dan* wrote:

The glorious victories recorded by the Laotian patriotic army
and people . . . are the most essential factors which determined . . . the splendid outcome of the Geneva Conference.
. . . It proves that many other problems can be solved by
peaceful negotiations provided the independence, freedom,
and peace-loving forces are united in the struggle against the
imperialist aggressors and warmongers.[73]

However, there is much evidence to suggest that North
Vietnam was deeply impressed both by the report of the
ICC condemning her actions in South Vietnam and by
the agreement reached over Laos at Geneva. The first
underlined the dangers attendant upon supplying un-
limited support to the Communist insurgents; yet without growing support it would plainly be impossible for
these insurgents to campaign successfully against the
South Vietnamese forces increasingly strengthened by
United States military assistance. The Laotian settlement was eminently satisfactory for the Communists in
that it had secured the withdrawal of United States
military personnel and had robbed SEATO of any pretext for interfering in Laotian internal affairs when the

[71] VNA, July 22, 1962.
[72] *Ibid.*, Aug. 2, 1962.
[73] *Nhan Dan*, July 24, 1962.

Pathet Lao Communists made their bid to assume full control of that country.

If similar agreements could be reached over South Vietnam, then a DRV victory would be virtually assured, for the United States soldiers would have to be withdrawn and could not return thereafter in the guise of SEATO forces. Better still, a neutral zone might be negotiated to cover Laos, South Vietnam, and Cambodia. Later on possibly Thailand and Burma might be added to it. Settlements of this kind would get rid of the only element capable of resisting Communist expansion — the United States — and the neutrality of the countries concerned could easily be left intact until the moment was judged opportune for their annexation, one by one, by the Communist bloc.

For the North Vietnamese leaders the prospect of a neutral South Vietnam had an added attraction. Since the latter could no longer object to trade with North Vietnam, South Vietnamese rice could be acquired, and the desperate food shortage in the North ended. During the latter part of 1962 and the early months of 1963, DRV propaganda campaigns appeared to be directed more toward extolling the advantages of a neutral South Vietnam than toward increasing the scale of insurgent military operations there. This propaganda urged the United States to withdraw and to allow the South Vietnamese to live in peace and neutrality; simultaneously it accorded maximum publicity to American "atrocities," laying particular stress upon the chemical defoliants being used and their allegedly terrible effects upon human beings and animals.

Nevertheless, military struggle continued unabated, for North Vietnam appeared to be convinced by the arguments she had advanced about the Laotian settlement. Negotiation leading to eventual neutrality, if it were to prove successful, had to be preceded by victorious armed struggle. Indeed, the struggle in South Vietnam might well have to be prolonged before the climate was ripe for negotiation because North Vietnam would demand greater concessions from an international conference than the Laotian Communists had done. Since Ho Chi Minh was anxious to negotiate neutrality only for South Vietnam and had no intention of removing the North from the Communist bloc, it would be necessary to induce in the United States a greater degree of weariness with the war and of frustration before she would agree to his demands. Consequently DRV exhortations to the insurgents in South Vietnam began to place increasing emphasis upon the long drawn out nature of the struggle and the impossibility of a quick victory.

SOVIET ECONOMIC ASSISTANCE

Following Nguyen Duy Trinh's four-week stay in Moscow an agreement was concluded with the Soviet Union for economic assistance to North Vietnam, but the very restricted publicity given to this agreement by the Vietnamese press and radio, coupled with the scant information divulged about the terms of the agreement, points to the conclusion that the North Vietnamese were disappointed by it. Strict silence was maintained about the total amount of the aid as well as the length of time over which it would be delivered, and no mention was made of the quantities of equipment, fuel, fertilizer, and the rest. This contrasts very strongly with the lengthy expressions of gratitude on the occasion of the 1960 aid agreement and with the very considerable detail which was then revealed. The Soviet aid, according to *Nhan Dan*, "will give us new possibilities of fulfilling the tasks set out in the first five-year plan," [74] which compares very oddly with the statement made by Nguyen Duy Trinh in 1960 that the "newly signed agreement constitutes a firm guarantee for the five-year tasks." [75] The impression is conveyed by the *Nhan Dan* article that most of the Soviet assistance would be in the form of technical advice, and the newspaper refers to Soviet "help" in the building of pumping stations for "80,000 hectares of land" and says that the Soviet Union would "advise" on hydropower development and "assist in expanding production" of a thermopower station. The only real enthusiasm expressed for the agreement came from Moscow Radio, which spoke in terms of high praise for Soviet aid in a broadcast to North Vietnam.[76]

Confirmation of DRV disappointment appears to be supplied by the high praise accorded to Chinese economic assistance to North Vietnam in two commentaries made only a week or so after the report of the Soviet aid agreement appeared in *Nhan Dan*. After expressing gratitude to the "Soviet Union, the Chinese People's Republic, and other brotherly socialist countries," Ha Vu Kinh went on:

In particular the Chinese People's Republic — the Chinese Communist Party, the government, and people — gave our people tens of thousands of tons of rice, millions of meters of cloth, and goods at the time of our taking over North Vietnam in 1954–55. Since then it has continued positively to

[74] *Nhan Dan*, Sept. 18, 1962.
[75] VNA, September (?) 1960. (Date omitted from author's copy of report.)
[76] Moscow Radio, Sept. 17, 1962.

assist us according to the needs of our economic and cultural stages, especially during the first five-year plan for building the material and technical bases for socialism.[77]

Writing in *Nhan Dan*, Nguyen Con, Vice-Chairman of the North Vietnam State Planning Commission, stated:

China has granted Vietnam free aid worth 900,000,000 yuan and long-term loans to the same value with conditions beneficial to us. China has also supplied us with complete sets of machinery and equipment to help build the material and technical bases of our economy.[78]

The reasons for these statements can only be guessed at, but a probable explanation would connect them with Soviet efforts to impose a greater measure of integration upon members of CMEA. It will be recalled that North Vietnam, angered by Soviet failure to support her condemnation of the ICC, failed to send observers to the previous CMEA Conference at which new measures were adopted. It remains unknown whether North Vietnam has been invited to accept membership in CMEA, but either from choice or necessity she has remained outside that organization. Increasing integration in Europe would have the effect of directing CMEA attention away from Asia, with a resulting fall of interest in economic aid to Asian bloc countries. It may be that North Vietnam refused an invitation to join, and that the unsatisfactory Soviet aid agreement was an expression of Soviet annoyance over her refusal, or possibly North Vietnam was not invited to membership and, as an outsider, became a less important candidate for Soviet economic assistance.

[77] Hanoi Radio, Sept. 25, 1962.
[78] *Nhan Dan*, Sept. 29, 1962.

CHINESE NATIONAL PEOPLE'S
COUNCIL DELEGATION VISIT

Since it has long been the custom of North Vietnam to go to considerable lengths to please visitors from abroad during their stay in North Vietnam, Vietnamese public statements must always be assessed in the light of this fact. During Soviet visits the Vietnamese convey the impression that their true sympathies in the Sino-Soviet differences are with the Soviet Union, and during Chinese visits the reverse is true. When the visitors have left, the statements made in their presence undergo a process of watering down which transforms them into expressions of neutrality, of sympathy for both sides. In spite of this tendency, and after making full allowance for it, a number of pronouncements by Vietnamese leaders during the visit of a Chinese National People's Council delegation under the leadership of Peng Chen display an unusually strong bias in favor of China. The phenomenon is the more surprising because the period of the visit coincided with a new flare-up in the dispute, with Peking issuing a new challenge to Moscow's leadership and North Korea expressing unqualified support for China. In circumstances such as these the almost unvarying practice of North Vietnam is to climb on to the fence and stay there, but on this occasion she showed less than her customary caution.

Albania and North Korea alone in the Communist bloc condemned the alleged Indian aggression against China along the northern border, and outspoken North Korean attacks on Yugoslav "revisionists" were rebroadcast by Peking Radio to Soviet audiences. North Vietnam was too circumspect to indulge in tactics of that kind, but she did send a delegation to Peking to participate in the celebration of China's National Day. Back in Hanoi Vietnamese leaders seemed to be throwing caution to the winds, with Xuan Thuy speaking of the "clearsighted leadership of the Chinese Communist Party and Chairman Mao Tse-tung," [79] Tran Duy Hung praising the "correct foreign policy of the Chinese government and people," [80] and the usually perspicacious Pham Van Dong outdoing all the others. Addressing the guests at a Hanoi reception for the visiting delegation, he said:

The Chinese People's Republic is a socialist country which has made constant and unreserved efforts to contribute to the consolidation of the solidarity and unity of mind of the socialist camp. . . .[81]

The effect of this statement in Moscow can be imagined, but what was the reason for it? Was it pique at the unsatisfactory Soviet aid agreement? Was it annoyance over some Soviet move, still unknown, which had caused the renewal of Chinese polemics? Whatever lay behind it soon paled into insignificance in the crisis which developed in the Communist bloc as a result of the Chinese attack upon India and the Soviet withdrawal of offensive rockets from Cuba. These were events which rocked the bloc to its foundations, and North Vietnam, like other Communist states, was obliged to adopt public attitudes over them.

[79] VNA, Oct. 1, 1962.
[80] NCNA, Oct. 7, 1962.
[81] VNA, Oct. 1, 1962.

THE SOVIET-CUBAN AND
SINO-INDIAN CRISES AND AFTER

5

THE CHINESE ATTACK ON INDIA
AND THE CUBAN CRISIS

With the launching of the Chinese attack against India,
Chinese press and radio engaged in a bitter denunciation
of India and the Indian leaders. China was wholeheartedly supported by Albania and North Korea. Moscow
maintained a cautious and embarrassed silence. The attitude of North Vietnam was indicated in a *Nhan Dan*
editorial which expressed anxiety over the blow the clash
had dealt to Asian solidarity but censured the perennial
villain, United States imperialism, stating that:

The United States imperialists and their satellites have tried
to draw to their side certain circles in India, slandered China,
and distorted its policy of peace and international cooperation in an attempt to drive a wedge between China, India,
and other countries.[1]

[1] *Nhan Dan*, Oct. 17, 1962.

Referring to Chinese demands for joint discussions of the border problem, it said:

This is a correct and unswerving stand of the Chinese government, which conforms both to sense and sentiment. The Vietnamese people approve the Chinese government's proposals to the Indian government to hold further negotiations.

Altogether it was a weak stand but probably contained just enough support for the Chinese to refute any charge that North Vietnam had failed to back another socialist state.

The visit to North Vietnam of a delegation of the NFLSV offered a welcome opportunity to avoid comment on Chinese actions in India, and for a whole week North Vietnam newspapers and Hanoi Radio devoted almost all available space and time to reporting the rallies for the NFLSV, the speeches made at them, the visits made by the delegation, and so on. All comment was reserved for the internal Vietnamese situation, with denunciations of President Ngo Dinh Diem and the United States. It was very natural and entirely safe. A week passed, and it was *Nhan Dan* which again published a DRV comment, but on this occasion support for China was more strongly expressed: "The Vietnamese people support the legitimate measures taken by the government and brotherly people of China to defend their national sovereignty." "The Indian government," it continued, "falsely accused China of invading its territory. . . ." [2] But the solution proposed was still "friendly negotiations." Reporting to the National Assembly on foreign affairs, Ung Van Khiem had nothing to add. He simply observed that the Vietnamese government and people

[2] *Ibid.*, Oct. 24, 1962.

"support the correct stand of China and eagerly hope that the Sino-Indian border question will be solved by negotiations between the two countries. . . ." [3]

Cuba was easier at the outset, and North Vietnam began in its customary fashion to tilt at United States "aggression," "provocation," "foolishness," and all the usual windmills. The pattern was familiar to the Vietnamese, and the pronouncements demanded neither thought nor ingenuity — merely clichés. A government statement of October 26 protested against the United States blockade of Cuba, and Truong Chinh the following day pledged National Assembly support for "the correct stand of the Soviet government expounded in its statement of October 23, 1962 on the Cuban question." Perhaps the Vietnamese might have carried the affair off successfully if they had restricted comment to Vietnamese spokesmen, but they rashly invited the Cuban Ambassador to comment, and he, in Hanoi, bluntly declared that United States allegations about Soviet rockets in Cuba were

. . . a fabrication to justify its policy of aggression in our country. The only military base on our territory at present is the United States base of Guantanamo. . . . The Soviet Union needs no bases other than those on its own territory. [4]

This comment was later to embarrass North Vietnam when the Soviet Union agreed to withdraw the rocket bases.

Timid endorsement of the stand of the Chinese government on the question of settling the border dispute with India was given by several DRV newspapers, [5] which

[3] VNA, Oct. 24, 1962.
[4] Ibid., Oct. 27, 1962.
[5] On Oct. 25, 1962 *Thoi Moi, Quan Doi Nhan Dan,* and *Bao Tan Viet Hoa* all published articles couched in similar terms.

expressed hopes for successful negotiations. Once more setting the pace for the others to follow, *Nhan Dan* changed its ground a week later and claimed to have identified an "Indian expansionist group clamoring for war, trying to instigate the masses to blame China, and sowing chauvinism." [6] The United States and Britain were of course blamed for supporting this group, but North Vietnam's pique over the Soviet attitude to the dispute was expressed for the first time. The Soviet Union was not mentioned by name, but the following extract leaves little doubt about the identity of the real target: "For their part, the revisionists in Yugoslavia also voiced support for this expansionist group in India and slandered China." The dispute, it said, "must be solved quickly by means of negotiations in the Bandung spirit."

Differences between the Soviet Union and China had meanwhile been further exacerbated by the Chinese attack on India, as was apparent from several public announcements made in Moscow and Peking. Moscow editorials on October 25 counseled a negotiated settlement on the basis of the Chinese proposals of the previous day, but they committed the unpardonable offense of failing to blame India for the fighting and, on the contrary, praised India for the part she had played in the "peace struggle." China's righteous indignation over the Soviet Union's failure to support her was expressed with no little bitterness in a *People's Daily* article that went on to attack the Soviet attitude toward national liberation movements in general. The article was followed by a whole spate of comment, both written and broadcast, explaining the correct behavior of socialist states in disputes affecting other socialist countries and by reports

[6] Editorial, *Nhan Dan*, Oct. 30, 1962.

that the Soviet Union intended to continue aiding India. Moscow comment reflected an even chillier attitude in the Soviet Union than hitherto, and less patience with China, but Chinese action was not condemned. These exchanges left little room for doubt about the mutual exasperation felt in the Soviet Union and China over the attack on India and the Soviet failure to support it. Any faint hopes that the Sino-Soviet dispute might still be resolved must surely have vanished in the unconcealed and growing hostility of the two Communist giants.

Developments in Cuba, which had at first appeared so straightforward, were suddenly complicated for the North Vietnamese by Khrushchev's agreement to withdraw Soviet rockets from that country. China was infuriated by his climb-down and lost little time in airing her feelings publicly, which meant that North Vietnam's commentators had once more to measure every word so as to avoid causing offense to the Soviet Union or China. A balance was achieved by according praise to the Soviet Union for safeguarding peace: "This attitude of the Soviet Union has upset the war provocations of the United States and makes its slander and distortion against the Soviet Union untenable. . . . These efforts of the Soviet Union have created a relaxed atmosphere." [7] Support was also pledged for Fidel Castro's five points: "The Vietnamese people unreservedly support the five proposals of Premier Fidel Castro. . . ." [8] The stand was repeated

[7] *Ibid.*, Oct. 31, 1962.
[8] *Ibid.* The "five points" refer to ending the United States blockade and other economic measures against Cuba; stopping actions carried on from outside Cuba aimed at undermining the Castro government; an end to "piratical" attacks from United States and Puerto Rican bases; stopping violations of Cuban airspace and territorial waters; and evacuation of the naval base at Guantanamo and return of Cuban territory occupied by the United States.

and elaborated day after day, and even the senile Vice-President, Ton Duc Thang, was placed on a public platform to give it his blessing: "Everybody knows the good will of the Soviet Union to settle the Cuban affair by peaceful negotiations." The Vietnamese people "will, together with the Soviet Union, China, and other brother countries of the socialist camp and the world's people, resolutely support Premier Fidel Castro's five point statement of October 28. . . ." [9] If North Vietnam had failed to condemn Soviet faintheartedness, at least it was at pains to show — for the benefit of Peking — that it did not trust the United States, and its declarations of support for Castro's five points grew more and more emphatic and were backed by large numbers of mass demonstrations in favor of Cuba. Once more the North Vietnamese position was one which could scarcely have pleased either the Soviet Union or China but which provided neither country with any solid grounds for objecting to it.

China's several offers to the Indian government to negotiate a solution to the border conflict, even if they were hedged about with conditions unacceptable to the Indians, at least gladdened the hearts of the North Vietnamese because they offered a completely safe subject for comment. Without examining the rights and wrongs of the Chinese armed attack, North Vietnam could castigate the Indians for refusing to accede to Chinese offers of peace, and they did so with a will. "In opposition to China's policy for peace are the policies of the Indian authorities to seize Chinese territories by force and their attitude of obstinately rejecting China's reasonable prop-

[9] Speech made on the forty-fifth anniversary of the October Revolution, VNA, Nov. 6, 1962.

osition." [10] The newspaper *Bao Tan Viet Hoa* "warmly endorses Premier Chou En-lai's reasonable proposals and his warm efforts to end the conflict . . . and to resume peaceful negotiations," [11] and the Vietnamese People's Army newspaper opined that the only "correct" way was to "stop the armed conflict" and "hold talks on the basis of the reasonable proposals of Premier Chou En-lai." [12] Most touching of all was the weekly paper *Thong Nhat*, which agreed that the Indian behavior must be bad because it had won the approval of the imperialists. The unilateral cease-fire imposed by China, subsequently followed by the withdrawal of the Chinese attackers, gave rise to profound relief in North Vietnam which showed itself in the torrents of praise for this "unselfish action." Ho Chi Minh himself sent letters to Liu Shao-chi and to the Indian President and Premier Nehru in which he congratulated the former and urged the two Indians to cooperate with China in finding a peaceful solution,[13] while the whole North Vietnamese press voiced similar sentiments at much greater length.

Great caution and circumspection had enabled North Vietnam to survive the crises of India and Cuba and emerge with her relations with the Soviet Union and China more or less intact, but the same cannot be said of these two leading Communist states. Chinese indignation over Soviet behavior was too great to be contained, and a fast swelling flood of propaganda was directed against the Soviet Union from Peking, culminating in mid-November with declarations which revealed that the

[10] *Nhan Dan*, Nov. 9, 1962.
[11] *Bao Tan Viet Hoa*, Nov. 9, 1962.
[12] *Quan Doi Nhan Dan*, Nov. 8, 1962.
[13] Text of letters in VNA, Nov. 23, 1962.

organizational break between the two parties was complete in every respect except that it had not been formally pronounced. Indeed, the *People's Daily* on November 15 went so far as to publish a guide for distinguishing Marxist-Leninists from revisionists and implied clearly that the Soviet Union passed all the tests for classification as revisionist. The following is a synopsis of the criteria:

1. Attitude toward imperialism: Revisionists "submit to imperialist pressure."

2. Ability to distinguish between anti-imperialist progressive nationalism and reactionary nationalism: Revisionists "support the reactionary nationalists."

3. Response to the national liberation movement: "The modern revisionists, represented by the Tito clique, are trying their utmost to benumb and undermine the national liberation movement."

4. Stand on the methods to be used in the transition to socialism: "The modern revisionists, represented by the Tito clique, preach the preposterous theory of so-called peaceful growth into socialism."

Prior to announcing the unilateral cease-fire, China engaged in a concentrated propaganda campaign that she has never equaled in sheer intensity, designed to convince the whole world, but particularly the unaligned neutralist countries, that the responsibility for the outbreak of hostilities was entirely India's and that China had no interest other than achieving a solution to the problem by peaceful negotiation. When, as a climax to this campaign, the cease-fire was proclaimed, Moscow reported it immediately but refrained from making any comment. Instead, the Soviets published Nehru's statements, to which they accorded the same prominence as those issued by

China. The breach between China and the Soviet Union by then was virtually open and complete.

COMMUNIST PARTY CONGRESSES

During the series of Communist party congresses in November and December 1962 there was further evidence of the gap separating the Soviet Union and China. The Soviet Union and her bloc supporters attacked Albania, and on December 10 *Pravda* published direct criticisms of the Chinese made by Togliatti and Novotný. But it is generally true to say that the proceedings at the congresses simply confirmed the view of relationships within the Communist bloc which had already been formed on the basis of evidence gleaned from other sources. By the time the Czechoslovak Congress ended on December 8, it was generally accepted that the antagonisms between the Soviet Union and China had reached such a stage of bitterness to make any *rapprochement* between the two countries seem out of the question; the matters of primary interest were the identification of parties supporting China or the Soviet Union or neither, and the future of the Communist bloc now that its leaders were divided.

In the past North Vietnam had shown that her principal objectives in the context of the Sino-Soviet dispute were twofold, the avoidance of irrevocable commitment to the side of either of the two main contestants and the ending of differences between them. By December 1962 even the most optimistic of the Vietnamese leaders must have been convinced that agreement was unattainable, but North Vietnam nevertheless clung grimly to its noncommittal path. Throughout the polemics of the different congresses the North Vietnamese delegation doggedly pursued a middle course and affected not to notice the dispute. The still incomplete information concerning these congresses indicates that the Vietnamese speakers refused to voice any criticism of Albania, which is precisely what informed observers would have expected.

The Sino-Soviet dispute was intensified by a speech made to the Supreme Soviet by Khrushchev on December 12 in which he stated "We equally absolutely do not entertain the thought that India wanted to start a war with China," and by the further improvement of relations between the Soviet Union and Yugoslavia. During President Tito's visit to Moscow in December, China, Albania, and North Korea maintained a nonstop barrage of vituperation against him and his country. The Soviet Union continued to lay heavy stress upon the need for settling East-West disputes by means of negotiations and never tired of citing the example of Cuba as proof of the success that could be achieved by mutual concessions and compromise.

A sidelight on the state of bloc relations was provided by the fiftieth anniversary of Albanian independence, celebrated in Hanoi at a reception given by the Albanian Ambassador to North Vietnam, Vasil Skorovoti. No doubt the citizens of Hanoi derived much useful information about the current state of play in the game of bloc relations by observing the attendance at this celebration, or rather the abstentions from it. North Vietnam was represented by a moderately strong delegation led by Vice-Premier Nguyen Duy Trinh and including Foreign Minister Ung Van Khiem, but the absence of President Ho Chi Minh, Premier Pham Van Dong, and other top leaders such as Le Duan, Vo Nguyen Giap, and Pham Hung was not without significance. Breaking with normal custom, the VNA report of the proceedings failed to mention the foreign ambassadors who attended but contented itself with a noncommittal "Diplomatic envoys of various countries also attended," [14] which lent credence to the reports emanating from Hanoi that only the Chinese and North Korean Ambassadors attended. The remaining embassies from bloc countries are said to have boycotted the affair altogether or to have been represented by their most junior officials. In making the principal speech, Nguyen Duy Trinh avoided all reference to the Albanian leadership and spoke only of the Albanian people.

Still more revealing was an incident that took place at the beginning of January 1963. Because the December meeting of the Supreme Soviet had discussed matters bearing on Sino-Soviet differences, it was virtually ignored by the North Vietnam press and radio. Only the briefest mention was made of the meeting, and no indication was given that it had dealt with such controversial questions. In an effort to force the DRV authorities into giving it greater publicity, Soviet Ambassador Suren Tovmasyan at the beginning of January held a press conference at Hanoi on the subject of the Supreme Soviet meeting. In addition to the customary press correspondents, the heads of the Indian and Indonesian diplomatic missions in North Vietnam were also invited to attend.

The Soviet Ambassador spoke about his country's economic development and foreign policy, making particular mention of Albania and Cuba, and then invited questions from those present. A few North Vietnamese asked about economic matters, after which the Chinese representative of NCNA made a lengthy statement disagree-

[14] *Ibid.*, Nov. 29, 1962.

ing with the Ambassador's remarks about Albania. He went on to advise Tovmasyan that it was useless to try to explain away the events in Cuba because everyone was well aware that the Soviet Union had surrendered completely to the United States. Smiling, the Ambassador reminded the meeting that he had asked for questions, not statements, and conceded that the Chinese journalist was entitled to hold what views he liked. He himself, he went on, did not try to impose his views on anybody, and he would be grateful if the Chinese would do the same. Nettled, the Chinese correspondent sprang to his feet and tried to continue his attack, whereupon Tovmasyan refused to discuss the matter further and declared the press conference over. The Chinese journalist loudly protested that he was not being treated as an equal, but the Ambassador and the embarrassed North Vietnamese hurriedly left the room while the Chinese correspondent continued to expostulate. Reports of the press conference appeared the following day but did not mention the incident. Members of the Soviet Embassy later called on the Indian and Indonesian Consuls General to explain what had happened because their terrified Vietnamese interpreter had stopped translating when the argument became heated.

THE NATIONAL FRONT FOR THE LIBERATION OF SOUTH VIETNAM (NFLSV)

The second anniversary of the founding of the NFLSV was the occasion of a double attempt at exploitation. While Moscow marked the occasion with no more than routine mention in the Soviet press, China availed herself of the opportunity to exploit the war in South Vietnam in her polemics against the Soviet Union. Her many comments at the time of the anniversary viewed the war being waged in South Vietnam as positive proof of the correctness of Mao Tse-tung's contention that revolutionary ardor will always prevail against imperialists and reactionaries with "superior weapons." The shining example of the South Vietnamese was contrasted with the precipitate withdrawal of the Soviets from Cuba. It is probable that the North Vietnam leaders had anticipated this Chinese exploitation of the anniversary and decided to exploit the Chinese in order to obtain at least some foreign recognition of the NFLSV as the rightful government of South Vietnam. Hanoi Radio broadcast a lengthy appeal from the NFLSV in which the following passage occurred:

In the past two years, and especially in recent days, the Front has scored many great diplomatic successes. Many governments and international organizations consider the Front the *legal representative* of the 14 million people in South Vietnam.[15]

This is a curious assertion because it is so patently untrue. No country, Communist or neutralist, has extended recognition to the Front as either the legal or *de facto* representative of the Southern people, and pains have always been taken on the occasion of a visit by one of the Front's representatives to make it clear that he is a guest of a nongovernmental organization — the World Peace Council, the WFTU, the Afro-Asian Solidarity Committee, or some such body — not of the government. The claim was repeated two days later, albeit in weaker form, in a message of greeting to the NFLSV from the DRV Fatherland Front, which claimed that Communist coun-

[15] Hanoi Radio, Dec. 17, 1962.

tries and "peace-loving peoples" have "in practice recognized the NFLSV as the legal representative" of the Southern people.[16]

The DRV attempt to secure recognition for the NFLSV proved unsuccessful. Summaries of the NFLSV appeal published in Peking and Moscow omitted the passage which alleged that the body was a legal representative. The version of the Fatherland Front greeting published in Peking made no mention of the representative function of the NFLSV, and Moscow ignored the greeting altogether.

VISITING DELEGATIONS

Although it is the almost invariable custom of North Vietnam to balance Chinese visits to North Vietnam by Soviet visits, the scale was tipped in favor of the Soviet Union during December and January. Two important Soviet delegations offset the two Chinese delegations which had come earlier, but these were followed by a state visit from President Novotny of Czechoslovakia, one of Khrushchev's staunchest supporters. The first to arrive was a surprisingly high-ranking military delegation under the leadership of General Batov, and the fact that its coming was announced only two days before it reached Hanoi gave it the appearance of having been arranged on very short notice.[17] Although some of its members made the usual well-publicized visits to places of interest, it became clear that the greater part of the delegation spent most of its time in North Vietnam working. General Batov himself passed almost the whole period of his stay working in the political office of the Vietnamese People's Army, while others appeared to be equally occupied. The length of the delegation's stay was two weeks, which is very much longer than that of a normal courtesy delegation. All these factors combine to create the impression that the Soviet military men came to North Vietnam to resolve some crisis or difficulty, probably a political one, in the Vietnamese People's Army, and it is probably significant that the DRV Commander in Chief, Vo Nguyen Giap, was not seen in public for a period of three months following the departure of the delegation. It is true that newspaper articles and letters bearing his name were published, but he himself did not appear. On the evidence available at present, however, it is impossible to reach any firm conclusions about the reasons for his disappearance.

Vo Nguyen Giap's major speech, delivered at an Army Day reception in Hanoi, was unexceptionable. It praised the Soviet Union for resolving the Cuban crisis and the Chinese for settling the Indian border crisis. A nice equilibrium was maintained when Giap said, "The Vietnamese people and People's Army value highly the great contributions of the Soviet Union, China, and the other socialist countries to the struggle for peace . . . ," [18] and he voiced a plea for bloc unity:

At the present time the Vietnamese people and the Vietnamese People's Army more than ever must hold high the banner of solidarity and unity of mind, the victorious banner of the international Communist movement, that is, the 1957 Declaration of the conference of representatives of the Communist and workers' parties and the 1960 Moscow Statement of 81 Communist and workers' parties, and uphold our soli-

[18] *Ibid.*, Dec. 23, 1962.

darity of proletarian internationalism with the peoples and armies of the Soviet Union, China, and other brother countries of the socialist camp.[19]

The visit of the Supreme Soviet delegation in mid-January was more routine and relatively uneventful, both sides making polite speeches and the Vietnamese making the expected concessions to the position of the Soviet Union. Only one speech appeared capable of causing any worry at all, and that was made by the leader of the delegation, Andropov. In it he accorded high praise to the Soviet Union and Khrushchev for solving the Cuban crisis, ignored the Indian fighting completely, and then went on to speak of peaceful coexistence. Underlining the correctness of the policy, he said, "The people who are devoting their energies to creative labor and turning their thoughts to a brighter future do not and cannot want war." He then expressed his happiness that "the North Vietnam government supports the Soviet proposals" on a wide range of subjects.[20] The content of this and other speeches made during the visit suggests that the delegation was bringing pressure to bear upon the DRV leaders to accept the Soviet rather than the Chinese position.

President Novotný, who visited North Vietnam later in January, undoubtedly argued the Soviet case, but it is far from certain that he achieved anything like the success credited to him in the Western press after the joint communiqué on his visit was published. Once again this was an instance of the DRV leaders going more than half way to meet the wishes of a foreign visitor to their country. Novotný's hand is discernible in the drafting of the

[19] *Ibid.*
[20] *Ibid.*, Jan. 16, 1963.

document, but Ho Chi Minh's influence is strong, even if it was overlooked by many readers. The importance of unity in the socialist camp is something which has never been underestimated by the North Vietnam regime, and the fact that the joint statement demands that an identity of views be achieved "through consultations" but adds that such consultations need "careful preparation" should cause no surprise to those familiar with DRV pronouncements. The statement endorsed the "proposals made by Comrade Khrushchev on behalf of the Central Committee of the CPSU, as well as of many brother parties, for the cessation of open polemics with a view to creating a favorable atmosphere for such a conference," but Chou En-lai had made just such an appeal for the avoidance of open polemics himself. There is a distinctly pro-Soviet flavor in the passages which state that "in the present international conjuncture, the most correct policy is the one of peaceful coexistence between countries with different social regimes," and that, "thanks to the persistent efforts and firm and correct measures of the Soviet Union . . . it was possible recently to stay the invasion of Cuba by the United States imperialist forces, to safeguard the fruits of the Cuban revolution, and to discard the imminent danger of a devastating nuclear war." Again the Soviet Union was called "the center of the socialist camp" and the CPSU "the tested and experienced vanguard of the international Communist movement." If, however, due allowance is made for the customary DRV concessions to foreign visitors for the sake of politeness, it will be seen that these remarks were carefully counterbalanced by reference to China as "recording big achievements in building socialism" and to joint "satisfaction at the Chinese government's decision of November 21, 1962 on the withdrawal of troops in the Sino-Indian border areas and its readiness to negotiate with the Indian side." In addition, both presidents declared their full support for "the just stand of the Chinese people on the liberation of Taiwan and the expulsion of the Chiang Kai-shek clique from that historical part of Chinese territory." [21]

Evidence that the joint communiqué was pro-Soviet in tone was mistakenly seen by much of the Western press in the document's publicity in the Soviet Union and in China's failure to mention it. It seems more probable that this Chinese display of pique was occasioned by Novotný's visit to North Vietnam and his transparent intention of canvassing the Soviet case rather than by the text of the communiqué itself. The Soviet Union followed up her temporary advantage by devoting many times more publicity than in the previous year to the thirteenth anniversary of the establishment of North Vietnam–Soviet diplomatic relations on January 30 and eulogizing the Lao Dong Party on the occasion of its thirty-third anniversary on February 3. China, which had devoted much time and space to the thirty-second anniversary, ignored the occasion completely. Obviously apprehensive over such a show of Chinese displeasure, North Vietnam hastened to placate her with an editorial describing both the Soviet Union and China as the "first" among countries supplying "disinterested assistance" to North Vietnam, and then went on to lay particular emphasis on Chinese aid which, it said, was the outcome of their "historic and geographical relations." [22]

[21] The text of the joint communiqué was issued by VNA on Jan. 29, 1963.
[22] *Nhan Dan*, Feb. 4, 1963.

THE EAST GERMAN PARTY CONGRESS
AND AFTER

The East German Party Congress in January 1963 provided evidence that a new and possibly critical stage had been reached in the Sino-Soviet dispute when the leader of the Chinese delegation to the Congress was subjected to the humiliation of catcalls and shouted abuse from the other delegates. This unprecedented behavior seemed to indicate that Khrushchev was offering China a choice between ending open polemics, which he demanded in his speech to the Congress, and *de facto* exclusion from the bloc. That an attempt was made to weight the proceedings heavily in favor of the Soviet Union was made apparent by Yugoslavia's TANYUG, which stated that the delegates from North Korea, North Vietnam, Burma, Thailand, and Indonesia — all countries which would have been unlikely to espouse the Soviet cause — were not permitted to address the Congress for "technical" reasons. North Vietnamese displeasure over the Congress is reflected in the very scant references made to it in the DRV press and by the lack of prominence given to these few reports. The speech of the Chinese delegate made it patently obvious that China had no intention of yielding one inch to Soviet pressures.

Later in January China demanded that the CPSU abandon her policy of *rapprochement* with Yugoslavia and made this a condition for the restoration of bloc unity.[23] An editorial in *Pravda* not only rejected this demand out of hand but also heaped scorn and ridicule on it.[24] Probably as a result of events at the East German

[23] Editorial, *People's Daily*, Jan. 27, 1963.
[24] *Pravda*, Feb. 10, 1963.

Party Congress and the implied determination of both the Soviet Union and China never to yield but to continue the dispute to the end, regardless of the consequences, North Vietnamese nerve cracked. For the first time the Politburo of the Lao Dong Party admitted to the people of North Vietnam that the socialist bloc had been split by disagreements, and appealed to the Soviet Union and China to restore unity in the interests of world communism.[25] This action alone shows beyond any possibility of doubt that the Sino-Soviet dispute had reached a pitch of intensity never before known, that the danger of a complete rupture of state and party relations between the Soviet Union and China was very great indeed. Throughout all the earlier wrangling the North Vietnamese leaders had taken considerable pains to conceal the differences from their people.

The Politburo statement is of such major importance that the full text has been included as Appendix A to this study. The document bears the stamp of having been hammered out at meetings of the Politburo in which the wide divergences of view among the individual members of that body were overcome under the strong pressure for unity imposed by Ho Chi Minh himself and by the danger of the disintegration of the international Communist movement. It is more revealing than any document hitherto published in North Vietnam, and its sense of urgency is unmistakable.

After a brief review of the world situation the statement admits frankly that Communist successes would have been greater if they had not been hampered by discord within the bloc. As long ago as January 1962, the document reveals, the Central Committee of the Lao

[25] VNA, Feb. 10, 1963.

Dong Party had dispatched secret letters to a number of other parties expressing its disquiet over the disagreements, urging that open polemics be abandoned and requesting that a meeting of Communist and workers' parties be convened to end the dispute. Despite subsequent temporary improvements, the situation had further deteriorated and was causing widespread concern. Understandable as the differences might be, they were detrimental to the cause of world communism and must be ended at a meeting of parties which would reach unanimous conclusions. With unaccustomed frankness the document then asserts that unity between the Soviet Union and China is the mainstay of bloc unity, mentioning these two countries by name, and it reiterates the same assertion in a subsequent passage. Following roughly parallel passages of praise for the Soviet Union and China, the statement reaffirms that the Central Committee of the Lao Dong Party has never ceased to strive for Sino-Soviet concord and bloc unity and concludes with three concrete proposals for remedying the existing unsatisfactory situation: an end of open polemics, a meeting of party delegates, and that the major responsibility for preparing such a meeting should devolve upon China and the Soviet Union. Shades of the customary North Vietnamese ambiguity and prevarication are apparent in the final paragraphs, where the document states that the international meeting should be carefully prepared — the Soviet view — and that it should take place speedily — the Chinese view. Nevertheless, the authors of the statement plainly made every effort to be impartial, and evidence of bias is apparent only in their demand that the international meeting of party delegates should reach unanimous, not majority, decisions. In this they run counter to Soviet wishes (the Soviet Union would have little difficulty in securing a majority at such a conference) and support Chinese demands.

It is not without significance that *Pravda*, which published a full translation of the statement on February 12, altered the text in only one place — the passage demanding unanimity. The Vietnamese "unanimous view" was translated as "single view," which implied that this could be reached by a majority decision and ruled out the possibility of factionalism. The day following the appearance of the statement *Nhan Dan* published an editorial in which full support was expressed for the Politburo document, but it made an even stronger affirmation that the Lao Dong Party had always worked hard for bloc unity:

. . . Our party has on several occasions expressed its opinions and proposed concrete measures for settling the divergences of views and strengthening unity within the international Communist movement. Our party's attitude, sincere and full of responsibility, has been welcomed by many brother parties.[26]

Once the Politburo statement had been published by VNA and supported by a *Nhan Dan* editorial, it might have been expected that the matter would have been allowed to rest there. Copies of the statement were undoubtedly distributed widely and studied endlessly at political meetings. That is the normal method of introducing new party policies to the people of North Vietnam, but only the published and broadcast materials reach the outside world. The local study groups work on unsung and almost unnoticed. However, on this occasion it would seem that the admissions contained in the statement had a shocking effect inside North Vietnam even

[26] *Nhan Dan*, Feb. 11, 1963.

though most of the people must already have been aware of the differences within the bloc; but it is one thing to entertain one's own theories and quite another to have them officially confirmed and in such a way as to leave no doubt of the seriousness of the situation. The standpoint of the Lao Dong Party had been clearly defined, and little was to be gained, at least from the point of view of clarity, by publishing fresh articles or commentaries that might only confuse or blur the already sharp outlines. Curiously enough, however, a long article was published in support of the Politburo statement more than two weeks later, and its author was Vo Nguyen Giap, the most notoriously pro-Soviet North Vietnamese leader. The reasons for publishing such an article, as well as some of its more revealing passages, are worthy of closer study.

In his article[27] Giap disclosed for the first time that the unity of the Lao Dong Party had been threatened in the past. He wrote:

Our party has been struggling on two fronts against occasional irresoluteness, as well as from internal leftism and rightism, when adopting and carrying out the lines, strategy, and policy during each phase of the revolution and also when modifying the lines, policy, and form of the struggle.

Later in the article he admitted, "the base of the party seemed to be on the point of disintegrating"; and again,

During the land reform our party encountered a number of difficulties. However, it adopted a Leninist attitude, affirming success and criticizing mistakes. It asked its members to show a responsible attitude, to be conscious of organization and discipline, and to place the interests of the party and people above all else. This correct attitude united the

[27] VNA, Feb. 21, 1963.

ranks of our party and the difficulties experienced in this serious trial were surmounted.

These are very important revelations and made at what might appear to be the worst possible time, when the world Communist movement was split in two. The point of greatest significance is that all the differences disclosed are in the past and are followed by assurances of present unity. The most convincing reason for such disclosures is that the Politburo statement may not have been universally accepted in North Vietnam as representing the unified views of the whole Vietnamese Communist leadership but only of a faction. Such doubts concerning the authenticity of the leadership's unity would be most likely to abound among senior party members who are probably aware of disputes within the Politburo. Public revelation of hitherto undisclosed truths concerning these difficulties would help to demonstrate to the doubters the authenticity of the reconciliation implied by the sentiments of unity expressed in the statement, particularly when the source of the revelation is a leader of one of the major factions. This is the role that Giap's article appears to have played. It should perhaps be noted that it is a role the article could play whether Giap wrote it himself, either freely or under compulsion, or whether it was written by somebody else and published over Giap's signature.

Another important feature of the article is the exact balance maintained between the sections praising the Soviet Union and those praising China. So obvious is the parallelism between the two that in several places the wording is almost identical. Even the most casual reader could scarcely avoid being struck by it, as the following extracts illustrate:

Praise for the Soviet Union

"Our party always maintains its unshakable unity with the great CPSU. . . . Even during the twenties of this century the Vietnamese Communists turned toward the cradle of the revolution. . . ."

"Since then the Soviet Union has always helped the Vietnamese revolution in all aspects in a generous, disinterested, fraternal, and internationalist spirit."

"The Soviet Union is wholeheartedly helping our party and people in the building of socialism in North Vietnam, supporting the valiant struggle of our compatriots in South Vietnam, and our entire people's just struggle for the peaceful reunification of the country, and approving and supporting our struggle for the correct implementation of the Geneva agreements to safeguard peace in Indochina and Southeast Asia."

Praise for China

"Our party is deeply indebted to the great CCP. Both from the historical and the geographical points of view, the Vietnamese revolution and the Chinese revolution were always closely related."

"Since the first days of the founding of our party . . . the Vietnamese Communists have enjoyed the wholehearted assistance, full of proletarian internationalist spirit, of the brotherly CCP and Chinese people."

"Since the restoration of peace, the Communist Party, government, and people of great China have wholeheartedly helped our people in the building of socialism in the North, fully supported the valiant struggle of our compatriots in the South and our entire people's just struggle for peaceful reunification of the country, and approved and supported our struggle for the correct implementation of the Geneva agreements to safeguard peace in Indochina and Southeast Asia."

The objective of this nice balance is to demonstrate to all readers that Vo Nguyen Giap, well known for his sympathies with the Soviet Union, considers the danger to world communism so great that he is prepared to overcome his own personal inclinations and to regard China and the Soviet Union as entirely equal for the sake of achieving Communist bloc unity. In further support of the unifying purpose of the Politburo statement, much of it was reiterated in the rest of the article, and its three concrete proposals were repeated verbatim.

North Vietnam used the anniversary of Karl Marx's death on March 14, which it had virtually ignored in past years, as a peg on which to hang several more important speeches and published articles concerning the Sino-Soviet dispute. All had the same form. They commenced with a brief history of communism from the time of Marx to the present day and followed that with praise for the Soviet Union and China. Next came remarks about differences in the Communist bloc and the urgent need for resolving them and cementing unity. A common feature is the omission of any mention of Stalin, which produced an unfamiliar imbalance in the historical accounts of communism. Yet another common feature is the attack on revisionism, described as the "main danger," on reformism, and on rightist tendencies, with leftist deviations and dogmatism receiving considerably less censure. Surprisingly outspoken about these latter questions, in view of the recent attempts at impartiality, was a *Nhan Dan* editorial that said:

Those who propagate revisionism are seeking by all means to make people recognize the necessity or possibility of realizing a "class concord" between the working masses and the magnate capitalists, between the oppressed peoples and the imperialists. The path of revisionism is but one that aims to divert the Communist and workers' movement from the orbit of scientific socialism. . . . Their [Yugoslav] activities have done much harm to the solidarity and unity of the international Communist movement.[28]

The clue to the reasons for this spate of comment is almost certainly to be found in the outspoken criticism of revisionism.

Since the visit of President Novotný to North Vietnam, China had showed her displeasure with the Vietnamese by not publishing or commenting upon the major happenings in North Vietnam. It may be that this displeasure was occasioned by the unusually long visit of the Soviet military delegation or by that of Novotný, or it may have arisen from secret exchanges within the bloc which have never been made public. Whatever the reasons, there can be no doubt that during the early months of 1963 the Chinese were displeased with the North Vietnamese. Suddenly, without any prior warning or indication that relations between the two had improved, the *People's Daily* devoted one and a half pages to the full texts of the following four documents:[29]

1. The February 10 statement on the solidarity of the international Communist movement issued by the Politburo of the Central Committee of the Lao Dong Party.

2. The joint statement made by Ho Chi Minh and Novotný, which had been published by VNA on January 29.

3. The February 11 *Nhan Dan* editorial entitled "Solidarity Is the Guarantee of All Our Victories."

4. An article in the March issue of *Hoc Tap* commemorating the anniversary of Karl Marx's death, entitled

[28] *Nhan Dan*, Mar. 13, 1963.
[29] *People's Daily*, Mar. 12, 1963.

"Reinforce the Solidarity and Unity of the International Communist Movement and the Socialist Camp." [30]

The abrupt change in the Chinese attitude strongly suggests that a secret bargain had been struck between the leaders of the two countries, and subsequent events make it possible to guess the nature of this bargain. It is a reasonable assumption that the cause of Chinese displeasure was the presence of Khrushchev's protagonist, Novotný, in a neighboring Asian Communist state and, to a lesser degree, the pro-Soviet tone of Vietnamese statements made during his visit. In order to placate the Chinese, North Vietnam utilized the anniversary of Marx's death as an occasion to publish a number of pronouncements more favorable to the Chinese standpoint, but this action redressed no more than part of the balance. The main Chinese grievance remained. Only when the North Vietnamese leaders agreed to invite the Chinese Head of State, Liu Shao-chi, to pay a formal visit to North Vietnam did Chinese anger abate. It is probable therefore that North Vietnam issued an invitation to Liu Shao-chi to pay a state visit to North Vietnam and that normal relations between the two countries were restored on or immediately before March 12, 1963.

The invitation to Novotný to visit North Vietnam was regarded in the Soviet Union and China as an important Soviet advantage in the Sino-Soviet dispute, for it pro-

[30] Major DRV pronouncements to mark the anniversary of Marx's death include: a speech by Le Duan, First Secretary of the Party, on Mar. 13 at Hanoi, reported by VNA on Mar. 14, 1963; a speech by Nguyen Chi Thanh, Politburo member and former Head of the Political Department of the Vietnamese People's Army, at Hanoi on Mar. 13, reported by VNA on Mar. 14, 1963; editorial, "The Name and Work of Karl Marx Live Forever," *Nhan Dan*, Mar. 13, 1963; editorial in *Hoc Tap*, Mar. 1963.

vided an opportunity to state the Soviet case in that un-committed Communist country and might be expected to suggest to the non-Communist world that the Viet-namese Communists were favorably disposed toward the Soviet Union. Viewed in that context, Chinese annoy-ance over the affair was not unreasonable. A visit to North Vietnam by the Chinese Head of State offered the double advantage of permitting him to undo the effects of Novotný's trip and at the same time of reminding the Soviet Union that Chinese influence in North Vietnam remained strong and could not be ignored. The Chinese, well aware of the Vietnamese habit of making statements favorable to their current foreign visitors, felt that they could be sure of some distinctly pro-Chinese pronounce-ments by Vietnamese leaders. The Vietnamese them-selves must have regarded the visits of both Novotný and Liu Shao-chi as great embarrassments impossible for them to escape, and occasions on which they would have need of all the political skill at the command of Ho Chi Minh.

THE STATE VISIT OF LIU SHAO-CHI

News of Liu Shao-chi's impending visit was not made public in North Vietnam for some weeks, being finally released by the Ministry of Foreign Affairs on April 27.[31] The delay was presumably intended to conceal the rea-sons underlying the sudden resumption of cordial rela-tions by the Chinese. Meanwhile, the North Vietnamese concentrated upon the acute difficulties facing them in their internal affairs, particularly in the sphere of agri-culture. The war in South Vietnam was also a matter of

[31] Ministry of Foreign Affairs communiqué, VNA, Apr. 27, 1963.

great concern, for the tide had turned against the Communist insurgents, and new measures would have to be adopted if the deterioration in the situation was not to accelerate. For that reason pressures were increased in Laos, where the Pathet Lao began a series of attacks against neutralist positions and received considerable DRV assistance in these operations.

After the spate of speeches bearing on the Sino-Soviet dispute which marked the anniversary of Marx's death, very little mention was made of the subject. Early in April, however, a major speech given on March 13 by Le Duan was published.[32] Only a brief and uninformative reference to this speech had previously been made by VNA, but the text now published proved so much to the liking of the Chinese that it was reprinted in full by the *People's Daily*, in which it filled two whole pages, and broadcast by NCNA.[33]

Rejecting Khrushchev's emphasis on economics as opposed to politics, Le Duan argued that "the proletariat has no alternative but to use violence to demolish the bourgeois state apparatus and to establish one of its own"; hence the political struggle "is of cardinal and decisive significance. Economic and ideological struggles must serve the purpose of helping to bring about the victory of the political struggle." Peaceful evolution into socialism, a theory that had won some favor in the Soviet Union, was given no more than lip service by Le Duan when he wrote, "That is why the working class and Marxist-Leninist parties, while seeking to make revolution by peaceful means, must make active preparations

[32] Le Duan, "Let Us Hold High the Revolutionary Banner of Creative Marxism to Lead Our Revolutionary Cause to Complete Victory," *Hoc Tap*, Apr. 1963.

[33] NCNA, Apr. 15, 1963, and *People's Daily*, Apr. 16, 1963.

for the seizure of power by violence." He also condemned aid of the kind supplied by the Soviet Union to bourgeois nationalist regimes such as those of India and Egypt: "Experience has proved that to advance along the non-capitalist road a nationalist country internally must depend in the first place on a strong Marxist-Leninist party." Yugoslavia and the Yugoslav revisionists were the targets of an outspoken attack which concluded that "a thorough exposure of the Yugoslav revisionists is a requirement essential to the smooth progress of the people's revolutionary cause in nationalist countries." The most curious feature of this speech was not, however, its content (a secret DRV directive in early March appears to have ordered that speeches and articles adhere closely to the Chinese line) but its timing. Possibly the publication was delayed until April to provide the Chinese with an earnest of continuing North Vietnamese good faith and to eliminate any doubts they may have had on that score.

A report by Pham Van Dong to the DRV National Assembly at the end of April [34] dealt with a wide range of subjects, but the section concerned with foreign policy seemed specifically designed to sound the keynote for Vietnamese utterances during the forthcoming visit of Liu Shao-chi, which had been announced at the time the report was made. Unity of the Communist bloc and good relations between North Vietnam and both the Soviet Union and China were themes which occupied the opening part of the report, and Dong was "happy to note that CPSU and CCP had exchanged letters with a view to advancing toward talks between the two parties." After stressing the political importance of Liu Shao-chi's visit,

[34] VNA, May 2, 1963.

he indicated the three issues on which North Vietnamese support for China could be expressed. China, he declared, was assured of full support in the struggle for the liberation of Taiwan, in her demand for a seat in the United Nations organization, and in her border dispute with India. It is interesting, if not entirely surprising, to note that these three matters were subsequently included in almost every North Vietnamese utterance during the Chinese visit. Cuba, it would also seem from Dong's report, had no longer been saved from the United States aggressors by timely Soviet action. The Cuban people were now "standing beside the Soviet Union, China, and other socialist countries." No comment was offered on Soviet behavior in this regard, but North Vietnam declared her support for the five points enunciated by Fidel Castro. A number of other matters were similarly dealt with, and several references were made to the nationalist countries of Asia, Africa, and Latin America in anticipation of possible Chinese mention of her proposed conference of three continents.

Preparations for the Chinese visit were on a scale never before witnessed in North Vietnam; they had about them a feeling reminiscent of Vietnamese preparations for the visit of a Chinese viceroy in the old days of Imperial China. In addition to all the flags, the streamers, the triumphal arches, the speeches on Chinese achievements, the performances of a Chinese circus, and the rest, the DRV Minister of Culture, Hoang Minh Giam, and the Ambassador to China, Tran Tu Binh, traveled to Kunming in order to accompany the visitor on his journey to Hanoi. Press and radio poured out volumes of the most obsequious flattery of China, and undoubtedly the DRV leaders waited in trepidation, hoping that Liu Shao-chi would exercise some restraint so as to avoid compromising them too badly.

At the banquet on the first evening Ho Chi Minh indicated how far North Vietnam was prepared to go to meet Chinese requirements when he offered support for China over Taiwan, the Indian frontier dispute, and the United Nations issue and ended with a strong plea for bloc unity. For his part, Liu made a polite and innocuous reply. There were no references to matters in dispute between the Soviet Union and China. Calm prevailed throughout the second day, too, but it was the tense, expectant calm that precedes a storm; and the storm broke dramatically when Liu Shao-chi spoke at a mass rally in Ba Dinh Square, Hanoi, on the morning of May 12.

Soviet attitudes and policies came under heavy attack from the Chinese leader, who, after attributing the favorable world situation to "long and repeated trials of strength and struggles on a world scale between the socialist camp and the people of the world on the one hand and imperialism headed by the United States and its lackeys on the other," [35] went on to belabor the policy of peaceful coexistence. He said:

The foreign policy of socialist countries must not be reduced to the single aspect of peaceful coexistence. Peaceful coexistence refers to relations between socialist countries and capitalist countries. It must not be reinterpreted at will or stretched to apply to relations between the oppressed and oppressor nations or between oppressed and oppressor classes. Peaceful coexistence must not be used to abolish the socialist countries' duty to support the revolutionary struggle of oppressed nations and people. The foreign policy of socialist countries, moreover, must not be used to supersede the revo-

[35] NCNA, May 12, 1963.

lutionary line of the proletariat of various countries and their parties.[36]

There was much more on this subject, but all of it followed similar lines. Liu also hinted strongly at one of the principal causes of Chinese resentment against the Soviet Union when he said:

The 1957 Declaration and 1960 Statement specifically stipulate that the socialist countries must respect each others' independence and sovereignty, treat each other with equality, refrain from interfering in each others' internal affairs, and cooperate on the basis of mutual benefit and help each other. If these principles are strictly observed instead of being violated, the unity of the socialist camp can certainly be strengthened.[37]

The whole speech was provocative and hard hitting, auguring ill for the outcome of the proposed discussions between the Soviet Union and China. The reactions of the North Vietnamese leaders to this Chinese polemic are not difficult to imagine. It is interesting to speculate why Tran Duy Hung, the Mayor of Hanoi, who spoke immediately before Liu Shao-chi at the mass rally, took the unusual step of omitting the CCP from the following passage of flattery for China:

As a powerful member of the socialist camp, the Chinese government and people have always indefatigably worked for the development of relations of friendship and fraternal cooperation with the other socialist countries in accordance with the principles of proletarian internationalism.[38]

Several possible explanations suggest themselves, but without more evidence it is fruitless to seek to explain the omission.

[36] *Ibid.*
[37] *Ibid.*
[38] *Ibid.*

Nhan Dan outdid itself during the Chinese visit. On the morning of Liu Shao-chi's arrival in Hanoi it appeared with the slogans, "We warmly welcome Chairman Liu Shao-chi on a visit to Vietnam" and "May Vietnamese-Chinese solidarity last forever" spanning its front page, printed in scarlet type and written in both Vietnamese and Chinese.[39] Two days later it published articles about the visit written by Vice-Premier Nguyen Duy Trinh, Vice-Minister of Culture Ha Huy Giap, and Ambassador to China Tran Tu Binh. The last named may have permitted his desire to carry out his directive to outstrip his respect for truth when he wrote:

. . . the Communist Party and government of China, which are always loyal to Marxism-Leninism and proletarian internationalism, are working energetically now, as in the past, for increased unity of the socialist camp and of the international Communist movement.[40]

Later *Nhan Dan* published an article commending Liu Shao-chi's "How to Be a Good Communist" to its readers and reminding them that the revised edition had now been published by the Su That Publishing House.[41]

The second of Liu's two major speeches in North Vietnam was delivered to a meeting at the Nguyen Ai Quoc Party School, and on that occasion he appeared to cast restraint to the wind when voicing what must surely be considered one of his bitterest attacks against the Soviet Union. Few could have entertained any doubts about the identity of the "certain people" when he said: "Now there are certain people who always stress their assistance

[39] *Nhan Dan*, May 10, 1963.
[40] *Ibid.*, May 12, 1963.
[41] *Ibid.*, May 14, 1963.

to others and disown others' assistance to them. This is flying in the face of facts. This is not a Marxist-Leninist attitude." [42] His strongest words, however, were reserved for the "modern revisionists," a term that he was certainly not applying solely to the Yugoslavs. He said:

The international Communist movement is now in a crucial period of the utmost importance. An acute struggle between the Marxist-Leninists and the modern revisionists is proceeding on a world-wide scale over a series of important problems of principle. The polemics are centered on whether the people of the world should carry out revolutions or not, and whether proletarian parties should lead the world's people in revolutions or not. The course of this struggle has a bearing on whether the entire cause of the proletariat and working people throughout the world will succeed or fail, and on the destiny of the whole of mankind. On questions of such an important struggle of principle, we cannot act as onlookers or follow a middle course.

The modern revisionists, donning a cloak of Marxism-Leninism, are actually wantonly adulterating Marxism-Leninism, emasculating Marxism-Leninism of its revolutionary soul, repudiating the historic necessity for proletarian revolution and proletarian dictatorship in the period of transition from capitalism to communism, negating the leading role of the proletarian party, substituting hypocritical bourgeois "supra-class" viewpoints for Marxist-Leninist viewpoints of class analysis, and substituting bourgeois pragmatism for dialectical materialism. They are trying their utmost to benumb the revolutionary will of the working class and tamper with the essential contents of socialism and communism as strictly defined by Marxism-Leninism in an attempt to preserve or restore capitalism in reality. Under such circumstances, the militant task of all Marxist-Leninists is not to evade the challenge of modern revisionism but to unite to smash its attack completely. In defense of the purity of Marxism-Leninism, hold aloft the red banner of revolution, and show

[42] NCNA, May 15, 1963.

the proletariat and working people the correct direction for struggle and the road to victory.[43]

The foregoing passage is self-explanatory, needing no commentary, but Liu's attack went even further. Following a scathing passage describing "how modern revisionists distort and tamper with Marxism-Leninism," he went on:

The many propositions advanced by the modern revisionists are not "creative developments" of Marxism-Leninism as alleged but a repetition and development under new conditions of the revisionist viewpoint of Bernstein, Kautsky, and other old-line revisionists. Most of their arguments were repudiated long ago by Marx, Engels, Lenin, and Stalin.[44]

Lest any member of his audience should be endowed with such quantities of natural optimism as still to look for agreement between the Chinese and Soviet representatives at their forthcoming meeting in Moscow, Liu Shao-chi ended his speech by demolishing all hopes for a speedy settlement. He said:

It is our firm belief that although the present struggle against revisionism will be a protracted and complicated one involving twists and turns, the all-conquering Marxism-Leninism will surely overcome revisionism and develop in the course of the struggle.[45]

Vice-Premier Chen I, who accompanied Liu Shao-chi to North Vietnam, made fewer pronouncements than is his wont, but he too hurled jibes at "certain people" who "publicize the view that one cannot oppose the United States and that opposition to the United States would

[43] *Ibid.*
[44] *Ibid.*
[45] *Ibid.*

lead to a great catastrophe." [46] He had no original contributions to make, however, and such statements as he did make simply parroted those already made by Liu.

Throughout the whole visit the North Vietnamese leaders exercised a guarded restraint in all they said and wrote, and even the most notoriously pro-Chinese of them remained within the boundaries already defined by Pham Van Dong in his report to the National Assembly. There is of course no way of knowing what transpired in the sessions of closed talks held with the Chinese visitors, but in their public behavior at least they presented a picture of party unity. The six days of Liu's visit may have seemed to them as though they would never end, but when they did, Ho Chi Minh was found at Gia-lam airport still eulogizing bloc unity:

The friendship between our two countries and parties, just as the solidarity and unity among all the countries of the socialist camp and all the fraternal Communist parties, is our most valuable asset and constitutes the firmest guarantee for all victories of the revolution.[47]

All of them could feel that they had emerged with some credit from a difficult and embarrassing situation and in the face of no little provocation.

The tone of the joint statement of Liu Shao-chi and Ho Chi Minh issued at the conclusion of the visit was distinctly favorable to China on a number of issues. It described revisionism as the main danger to the international Communist movement and attacked Yugoslav revisionism as the concentrated expression of modern revisionist theories, going so far as to declare, "The Yugoslav revisionist clique has betrayed Marxism-Leninism

[46] *Ibid.*
[47] VNA, May 16, 1963.

and has led Yugoslavia out of the socialist camp." [48] The principle of attaining "unanimity" within the bloc instead of a "single view," with all its implications such as the right to indulge in factionalism and the rest, was endorsed by both signatories. Ho Chi Minh would appear to have expressed North Vietnam's approval for the Chinese development of nuclear weapons when he subscribed to the following view:

In the circumstances in which imperialism rejects disarmament and continues preparations for a nuclear war, it is highly necessary to strengthen the national defense might of the countries in the socialist camp, including the development of nuclear superiority of the socialist countries.[49]

China was described as having adopted a correct stand in her border dispute with India, and there was much else besides. Nevertheless, despite all the apparent approval for Chinese actions and policies, the joint statement provides evidence that Ho stubbornly resisted some Chinese pressures and agreed to express his support only up to a certain point. It is probable that there were disagreements between the two heads of state during the private discussions.

In view of the attacks upon peaceful coexistence made by Liu Shao-chi in the course of speeches made in North Vietnam, it is curious that the joint statement fails to express any condemnation of that policy. Again, although both Liu and Ho declared their wish to see bloc unity attained and opined that meetings offered the best way of achieving it, Ho Chi Minh alone expressed the opinion that the meetings would prove successful. He was again alone in stating that the CPSU and the Soviet Union

[48] NCNA, May 16, 1963.
[49] Ibid.

bore the greatest responsibility for re-establishing bloc unity. Liu Shao-chi, it would seem, deliberately disassociated himself from these views. Once again North Vietnam inclined heavily toward the side of the distinguished foreign visitor but had refused to go the whole way or to commit itself irrevocably to one side in the dispute. (A comparison of the joint statements issued at the conclusion of the Novotný visit and the Liu Shao-chi visit is given in Appendix B in order to provide concrete examples of the extent to which the North Vietnamese leaders will accede to the wishes of a visitor without finally abandoning their own uncommitted position.)

Comments by the two countries about the visit shed additional light upon their respective attitudes. Chinese satisfaction with the outcome is apparent from the publication of the joint statement together with the text of Liu Shao-chi's two major speeches in pamphlet form by the People's Publishing House on May 24. An assessment of the statement made by a *People's Daily* editorial [59] concluded that peace and final victory over imperialism could best be achieved by supporting the national liberation movements in Asia, Africa, and Latin America, thereby suggesting that the statement had condemned peaceful coexistence, which it had not. Indeed, the same editorial indulged in some journalistic sleight of hand by departing from the text and quoting Liu's outspoken attacks on peaceful coexistence as though they had formed part of the text. The final impression left with the reader of this article was that Liu's visit had secured an identity of views between China and North Vietnam on a number of questions in dispute within the Communist bloc.

For its part North Vietnam interpreted the statement

* *People's Daily*, May 23, 1963.

as a step forward toward bloc unity. The conclusion of the lengthy *Nhan Dan* editorial devoted to the joint statement ran as follows:

We are convinced that the strengthening of the solidarity and unity of mind between the two parties and governments will contribute to the vigorous development of the forces of the Vietnamese and Chinese peoples to build socialism successfully, thus actively contributing to the consolidation and strengthening of the solidarity and unity of mind within the socialist camp and the international Communist movement, of which the solidarity of the CPSU and the CCP and between the Soviet Union and China is the mainstay.[51]

The statement's bitter and uncompromising attack on Yugoslavia made it clear that on the issue of Yugoslav revisionism at least North Vietnam was at one with China and at variance with the Soviet Union. Indeed, Drago Kunc, a spokesman of the Yugoslav Foreign Secretariat, described the attack as an "extremely hostile act by the two responsible officials of the Chinese People's Republic and North Vietnam," and his government sent a formal note of protest to China. Yet this represented no major policy change on the part of North Vietnam, which had consistently criticized the Yugoslavs since the announcement of the Yugoslav Draft Program in May 1958. The only difference between this and earlier DRV pronouncements on Yugoslavia lay in the degree of severity in the wording of the criticism. A subsequent attack on that country, couched in language no less strong, was published in Hanoi a week after the departure of Liu Shao-chi.[52]

Nevertheless, North Vietnam lost no time before read-

[51] *Nhan Dan*, May 17, 1963.
[52] *Ibid.*, May 22, 1963.

justing the balance of her relationships within the bloc by assuring the Soviet Union of her undying friendship. The occasion was the thirteenth anniversary of the Vietnam–Soviet Friendship Association, and the Chairman of that body, Vice-President Ton Duc Thang, wrote a newspaper article in which he proclaimed: "The Soviet Union and Vietnam are brother countries in the great socialist family." [53] The greater part of the article was made up of variations on that theme, but the concluding paragraph stated once again the position of North Vietnam:

The stand of the Lao Dong Party and the DRV government is to strengthen unceasingly the unity with the Soviet Union, China, and other socialist countries, with neighbors, and with the forces of national independence, democracy, and peace in the world.[54]

The process of returning to neutral territory between the Soviet Union and China while retaining good relations with both was once more under way.

[53] *Ibid.*, May 23, 1963.
[54] *Ibid.*

CONCLUSIONS ★

6

LONG-TERM OBJECTIVES
OF THE NORTH VIETNAMESE COMMUNISTS

The clearest statement of the long-term objectives of the Lao Dong Party which has yet come to light is to be found in a secret party document captured by the French Expeditionary Corps in North Vietnam during the spring of 1952. Although this document is now 11 years old, there is no reason for supposing that the objectives it describes have been altered in any way. On the contrary, subsequent events in Indochina have all tended to confirm its contents.

On February 11, 1945 the Indochinese Communist Party was officially dissolved. It is now freely admitted by the Vietnamese Communists that in fact the party continued its existence and increased greatly in numbers and influence after that date. At a meeting held on February 11, 1951 the National Congress of the Indochinese Com-

munist Party decided that the party should reappear officially with the title Dang Lao Dong Viet Nam (Vietnamese Workers' Party). All these actions were taken
for perfectly valid reasons which do not need to be ex-
plained here, but the change of name from "Indochina"
to "Vietnam" caused numbers of Vietnamese Communists to have misgivings, for they imagined that the
change of name implied that Vietnam was proposing to
abandon her influence in Laos and Cambodia. To reassure these Communists, and to explain that the change
of name was no more than a temporary tactical expedient,
the Lao Dong Party issued the secret directive just mentioned.

Although the captured directive contains much invalu-
able information concerning the Indochinese Communist
Party and the Lao Dong Party, the only sections directly
relevant to this study are those that state the reasons for
the replacement of the Indochinese Communist Party
by three national Communist parties and the ultimate
objectives of those parties. Very briefly, the reason for
the change was to avoid causing offense to the susceptibilities of Laotian and Cambodian nationalists engaged
in fighting against France. The latter were well aware
that all the senior positions in the Indochinese Communist Party were occupied by Vietnamese, and they also
knew that their own resistance movements were under
the direction of the Indochinese Communist Party. Lest
they resent Vietnamese direction of their movements,
national Communist parties were formed. The captured
directive states that the Laotian and Cambodian Communist Parties continued to receive their orders from the
former Indochinese Communist Party, but they did so
secretly, and the overt leadership of the two parties was

in the hands of Laotians and Cambodians. The captured directive continues: "But later on, when conditions permit this to be carried out, the three revolutionary parties of Vietnam, Cambodia, and Laos will be reunited to form a single party." [1]

Thus the ultimate aim of the Vietnamese Communist leadership is to install Communist regimes in the whole of Vietnam, in Laos, and in Cambodia, after which they will re-form a single Communist party. This one party will then rule the three countries. The captured directive does not state, but strongly implies, that the single party will be controlled by Vietnamese Communists in the same way the Indochinese Communist Party was.

At the present time the Vietnamese Communists are masters of North Vietnam only, but they are engaged in a war of subversion aimed at bringing South Vietnam under their control and are providing help in arms, men, and political direction to the Laotian Communists in the Pathet Lao. These activities are directed toward the achievement of the objectives stated in the captured document, and there are strong indications that the objectives have been neither changed nor modified. This can be said despite shifts in the tactics used to gain these objectives. For example, the northern half of Vietnam was not economically self-sufficient in 1954 when the Communist regime assumed control, and has still not achieved self-sufficiency today despite the aid supplied by other members of the Communist bloc. Hence North Vietnamese actions and tactics for achieving the stated objectives of the Lao Dong Party have been influenced

[1] Directive of the Lao Dong Party, dated Nov. 1, 1951 and classified "Top Secret."

by the state's economic needs, particularly by her insufficient agricultural production.

Before passing from this section on the long-term objectives, it is worth citing one more short extract from the captured directive. Part C, section 5 reads: "Not only is it our duty to aid the revolutionaries in Cambodia and Laos but we must also aid the revolutionary movements in the other countries of South East Asia, countries such as Malaya, Indonesia, Burma, etc."

THE ECONOMIC SITUATION

The most serious difficulty affecting the internal situation of North Vietnam in the spring of 1963 was the very grave shortage of food. Nghiem Xuan Yem, the then Minister of Agriculture,[2] struck a note of despair when he reviewed the agricultural developments during 1962. He said:

Between the spring of 1961 and the winter of 1962 many natural calamities caused great damage and posed obstacles for the execution of the agricultural production plan. Toward the end of last year sudden, repeated, and heavy rains prevented the practice of the "ai" cultivation method for the fifth month crop and caused the winter secondary and industrial crops to fail. The recent tenth month crop was damaged by drought and stagnant water, causing the cultivated acreage to be reduced by 20,000 hectares. Typhoons and sudden rains which occurred toward the end of September caused damage to early crops, paddy crops, secondary crops, and fruit trees in many provinces.[3]

[2] He was removed from the post in Jan. 1963.

[3] Broadcast by Hanoi Radio, Dec. 21, 1962. The two principal rice crops in North Vietnam are called the fifth month and the tenth month, after the dates of the harvesting. Of these the larger and more important crop is the tenth month.

He went on to speak of the "alarming situation of the tenth month crop" and, a little later, of the "alarming reduction of our cattle herds the previous year." [4] Earlier in the year, in an effort to alleviate the food shortages, which has about it the signs of desperation, the Premier's Office introduced an order dated August 6, 1962 that obliged civil servants, factory workers, construction workers, school children, soldiers, policemen, and others to grow food in their spare time on any vacant pieces of land in or around their places of work. Part of the order read:

Each [governmental] organization, school, construction site, factory, and unit of the Army and People's Armed Police must devote any spare time and all spare pieces of land to [food] production in order to ensure that each cadre and public service student produces annually a certain average quantity of food for his own consumption — 10 kilograms of vegetables and more meat to improve his daily diet.[5]

The biggest reshuffle of the government since the Communist regime assumed control took place in January 1963, and the most important changes affected the administration of agriculture. Since then a further and very grave deterioration has occurred. A directive of the Central Committee Secretariat of the Lao Dong Party issued on February 1 announced that a drought of unprecedented intensity had been going on for two months and still showed no signs of ending. Two of the measures ordered in this directive will suffice to illustrate the gravity of the agricultural situation:

In the delta, the middle region, and Thanh-hoa, the spring transplanting [of rice] must be completed by February 10,

[4] *Ibid.*
[5] Hanoi Radio, Aug. 6, 1962.

1963. In a number of coastal areas, where the people must wait for water currents, the completion of transplanting can be delayed until February 15, 1963. If transplanting cannot be carried out before these deadlines, it will be necessary to switch to other crops and struggle vigorously in order to cultivate [i.e., plow up] all the paddy fields where the transplanting cannot be achieved in time.

Where needed, they [the local authorities] may mobilize soldiers, policemen, and students to struggle against the drought.[*]

The drought continued unbroken well into April, and DRV press and radio reports about the situation show that civil servants and factory workers as well as soldiers, policemen, and students were sent into the countryside to help in trying to salvage something from the wreckage. Even Ho Chi Minh himself found time to carry some symbolic buckets of water and pour them into parched rice fields. Every other internal problem of North Vietnam has paled into insignificance beside the disastrous agricultural situation. It is difficult to see how famine on a national scale can be averted, for no country in the Communist bloc is in a position to send supplies of rice to North Vietnam, and offers of help from the West would almost certainly be refused for political reasons.

With each passing year the internal situation in North Vietnam becomes increasingly difficult. Certainly industrialization is going on with aid supplied by the rest of the bloc, but progress has been disappointingly slow, and in the last resort all else depends upon the ability of the North Vietnamese people to feed themselves. The instances of bad feeling between the North Vietnamese and the bloc technicians in North Vietnam are manifes-

[*] The text of this directive was broadcast in Hanoi Radio's domestic service in Vietnamese on Feb. 1, 1963.

tations of Vietnamese disappointment with the achievements of bloc aid, but there is also evidence of the exasperation felt by these visiting Communist technicians
when dealing with the Vietnamese. Gérard Tongas has
cited specific examples of this[7] and noted that it was particularly prevalent among East German technicians. Since
the publication of Tongas' book, I have listened to com-
plaints made by leading Chinese Communists about the
Vietnamese to some of my personal friends. The Chinese
accused the North Vietnamese of arrogance, unwilling-
ness to learn, refusal to carry out orders, and an unshakable conviction that they themselves know better than
any foreigner. I have received no such first-hand reports
regarding the attitude of the Soviet technicians, but I see
no reason to doubt that the Soviets too have shared the
experience common to the Chinese and East Germans.

For all these reasons it has become more and more
imperative for the leaders of North Vietnam to find some
solution to their immediate economic problems and to
find it quickly. The armed insurrection in South Vietnam
has shown no prospects of success in the foreseeable future, and for some months North Vietnam has been
calling for the setting up of a neutral state in South Vietnam. This might well delay Communist annexation of
South Vietnam, but it would offer the advantage of immediate trading relations between the Northern and
Southern zones so that North Vietnam could purchase
Southern rice. The major obstacle standing in the way of
such a solution is North Vietnam's insistence that neutral status should apply only to South Vietnam and not
to herself. Even if the government of President Ngo Dinh

---

[7] Gérard Tongas, *J'ai vécu dans l'enfer communiste au Nord Vietnam
et j'ai choisi la liberté* (Paris: Les Nouvelles Editions Debresse, 1961).

Diem should be replaced, no representative government of South Vietnam would be likely to agree to such unequal terms.

The internal problems facing North Vietnam are formidable indeed. In the early years of the state's existence her leaders were confident that, however great the difficulties they might have to face, they could always rely upon the support and assistance of the Communist bloc to ensure that they overcame them successfully. That confidence no longer persists. Today the divisions within the bloc are so great that a reconciliation between the Soviet Union and China no longer seems possible. The most that can be hoped for is an uneasy compromise solution, a papering over of cracks, which could at best be only temporary. Under these conditions North Vietnam's leaders must be as apprehensive about external problems as they are over their internal situation.

THE ATTITUDE TOWARD
SINO-SOVIET DIFFERENCES

The attitude of North Vietnam toward the differences that divide the Soviet Union and China, as will already have become apparent from this study, is one of wishing to avoid a final and irreparable breaking off of all relations between these two countries. It is plain that the time when a resolution of the differences was still possible has already passed and that there is no longer any hope of restoring to the Communist bloc the unity which persisted only a few years ago and which for the North Vietnamese Communist leaders would have been the perfect solution of their problems. When the perfect proves to be unattainable, the second best is sought, and that, for

North Vietnam at least, is the preservation of some relationship, no matter how tenuous, between the Soviet Union and China.

The reasons for such an attitude can best be understood by imagining a situation in which these two leading Communist states had severed all links, all agreements, and faced each other as rivals for the leadership of world communism. In this situation it would immediately become necessary for each of the other Communist states to make a decision about which leader to follow. For the majority of these states deciding would not prove too difficult because most are already aligned with one or the other of the two leaders, although the enforcement of the decision upon all members of their national parties would be far from easy. Communist parties in non-Communist countries would be placed in an extremely delicate position which there is no need to examine here. For North Vietnam the choice would be agonizing because, no matter which bloc she decided to join, the end would be the same — disaster.

Let us suppose that Ho Chi Minh still held the reins of power in North Vietnam and elected to follow the Soviet Union on the grounds that Soviet and East European aid was indispensable for his country. Aid would no longer be able to cross China and would be obliged to follow the long sea route. It would become subject to delays and reductions because it would depend upon what merchant shipping was available to the Soviet Union. Chinese aid would be discontinued immediately, and the railways connecting North Vietnam with China would cease to have any value. Chinese technicians would be withdrawn, which would introduce disorder and chaos, especially if there were not sufficient technicians available from the Soviet bloc to replace them. North Vietnamese trainees and students would be returned from China, their courses incomplete, and it is doubtful whether all could be accommodated by the Soviet Union and her European partners even if the students should prove able to overcome the linguistic and other difficulties.

The foregoing economic disadvantages would be the least important, however, and would be heavily outweighed by political and military ones. The events in the last quarter of 1957 showed how strong was the pro-Chinese faction within the North Vietnamese leadership, yet at that time nothing more than a change of emphasis in the economic relations of the state was at stake. A final decision to break all ties with China, to replace friendly relations with hostility, would certainly bring about upheavals within the leadership very much more serious and far-reaching than those of 1957. Since Vo Nguyen Giap has never been a friend of China and his following within the Vietnamese People's Army is believed to be strong, in the last resort it is conceivable that the army might be used in support of Ho Chi Minh and the pro-Soviet faction. The use of force could ensure the supremacy of those loyal to the Soviet Union, but such a victory would be short-lived. Under circumstances such as these the pro-Chinese faction would probably appeal to China for military aid, possibly posing as the legal government of North Vietnam. The Soviet Union is too far away to be able to send sufficient forces to withstand a Chinese armed attack even if she were prepared to do so. Short of dropping nuclear bombs or rockets upon China, there is no way in which the Soviet Union could protect North

Vietnam, and it is safe to forecast that she would not resort to the use of nuclear weapons. A decision to remain loyal to the Soviet Union would therefore lead quickly to the ascendancy of the pro-Chinese faction and a reversal of the original decision. North Vietnam would then become entirely dependent upon China, for she could not be defended by the Soviet Union, and all Soviet or East European technicians would be obliged to leave. Aid other than Chinese would cease. China might for a time govern North Vietnam through Vietnamese puppets, but she would in all probability soon tire of that and initiate direct rule, making North Vietnam another province of China. When that happened, and Vietnamese adherence was assured, the Chinese would be under no further pressure to supply aid to the Vietnamese. Indeed, if former Chinese conduct is any guide, she would be more inclined to strip North Vietnam for the benefit of China.

Let us now suppose that Ho Chi Minh decided to ally himself with China instead of the Soviet Union. The decision would be followed by the departure of Soviet and East European technicians and a cessation of aid from these sources. China, for the same reasons as given in the previous paragraph would no longer have to compete with the Soviet Union to win Vietnamese allegiance, so there would probably be an end to Chinese aid. Sooner or later rule through Vietnamese puppets would give way to direct Chinese rule, and North Vietnam would become another province of China. Once more the probability is that North Vietnam would be stripped for the benefit of China.

Ho Chi Minh is now in his middle seventies, but he

is still the repository of all political power in North Vietnam. When he departs from the Vietnamese political scene — and this cannot now be long delayed — a power struggle will almost certainly ensue. There is little point in trying to forecast the outcome at present, but the factional strife will be intense, and the Vietnamese People's Army may well be brought into it, with resulting bloodshed. In the present uneasy state of Communist bloc relations it is still just possible that the political disorders might be brought to a reasonable conclusion by means of pressures from other members of the bloc before too much damage had been done. Any such disorders, if they should break out when there were two hostile Communist blocs in existence, could scarcely avoid being exploited by both sides, and the results would probably be catastrophic for North Vietnam.

Few can doubt that so thoughtful a statesman as Ho Chi Minh has long foreseen all these possible consequences. However, he is almost powerless to stop the precipitate progress of the quarrel between the Soviet Union and China. As the Politburo statement of February 10 pointed out, North Vietnam has appealed for unity within the bloc, has pleaded for a meeting of Communist parties to settle differences, and has pointed out that the dispute is producing the most adverse effects upon the Communist cause throughout the world. Ho Chi Minh has clearly used all his own personal influence behind the scenes to resolve differences, but his efforts have been ineffective. There is little more he can do at this juncture except hope that matters will improve. As long as some links remain between China and the Soviet Union, North Vietnam will not be called upon to make the terrible decision about which leader to follow. Once those links have been severed, however, then the die will have been cast. North Vietnam will begin to slide down the slope that leads to Chinese domination or Chinese annexation.

Appendix A

TEXT OF STATEMENT OF THE POLITBURO
OF THE LAO DONG PARTY
CENTRAL COMMITTEE, FEBRUARY 10, 1963 [1]

In recent years the world situation has developed in accordance with the predictions of the Declaration and Statement of the meetings of representatives of Communist and workers' parties in Moscow in 1957 and 1960. The socialist camp has recorded new and great achievements in all fields in the building of socialism and communism and the defense of world peace. The national liberation movement continued to gain momentum, and the colonial system was disintegrating in quick succession. In the capitalist countries the struggle of the working class against monopoly capitalism has drawn in many more strata of working people and has become stronger with every passing day. The contradictions rending the world capitalist system have deepened further.

The imperialists, headed by the United States imperialists, have shown more and more clearly their cruel, aggressive, and warlike faces. They continued their policy of creating tension, feverishly carried on the arms race, prepared a new world war, sought by all means to repress the national liberation movement and to maintain colonialism in many forms, and schemed to sabotage the socialist camp and split the international Communist and workers' movement. However, they have met with the resolute struggle of the world's peoples, and the situation has become more and more disadvantageous to them and favorable to the people.

[1] VNA bulletin broadcast by Hanoi Radio, Feb. 10, 1963.

The struggle of the people of various countries for peace, national independence, democracy, and socialism could have won still greater successes and caused many more setbacks and difficulties to imperialism if the socialist camp and the international Communist movement had united and co-ordinated actions more closely. However, it is regrettable that discords have arisen between a number of brother parties.

In the face of this situation, in January 1962, the Central Committee of the Lao Dong Party sent letters to a number of fraternal parties expressing its concern and proposing that a meeting be held between representatives of Communist and workers' parties to settle the discord together and that, pending such a meeting, the parties cease attacking one another in the press and over the radio.

After that the situation was at times somewhat improved. However, over the recent period events took place which aggravated the relations between a number of fraternal parties. All the imperialists and reactionary forces in the world are rejoicing over this and are seeking by all means to take advantage of it in an attempt to aggravate this state of things still further. Meanwhile all the Marxist-Leninists, the broad masses in various countries, and many progressive people in the world have shown concern and sorrow.

The Lao Dong Party holds that in a situation wherein the Communist movement has become powerful, the Communist and workers' parties are carrying out their activities in very different conditions, and the development of the revolutionary movement has raised before the parties many complicated problems; hence the fact that one party holds different views on certain questions from another is something difficult to avoid.

Nevertheless such divergences of views should not be allowed to harm the fraternal unity among our parties. The unity of the Communist and workers' parties is the nucleus for uniting the revolutionary movement of peoples all over the world. In the face of the enemy, the imperialists, who are seeking by all means to split the international Communist movement, sabotage the socialist camp, and sabotage peace, we should endeavor all the more to strengthen solidarity. The interests of socialism, world peace, and the future of mankind make it essential for us to unite. Solidarity is the guarantee of all our successes.

Communists have all the necessary conditions to overcome divergences of views and firmly to maintain and enhance unity within their ranks. We have a common enemy — imperialism. We have a common ideology — socialism and communism. We have a common program — the Moscow Declaration of 1957 and the Moscow Statement of 1960. These declarations and statements have laid down principles on the strategy and tactics of the international Communist and workers' movement, rules guiding the relations among Communist and workers' parties, and methods to overcome divergences of views which may arise between parties — that is, to meet and consult one another in order to reach unanimous views. All Communist and workers' parties must most scrupulously respect all stipulations of these declarations and statements which have been recognized by all.

The Lao Dong Party holds that unity among the Communist and workers' parties of the countries in the socialist camp is of extreme importance for the unity of the international Communist movement, and that the unity between the Communist Party of the Soviet Union and the Communist Party of China, between the Soviet Union and the Chinese People's Republic, constitutes the mainstay for uniting the socialist camp as a whole.

The great Communist Party of the Soviet Union, the party of Lenin, is the vanguard of the international Communist movement. The Soviet Union is the first country to have carried out the socialist revolution, the country which has successfully built the first socialist society in the world, and is building communism. The victory of the October Revolution and the building of socialism and communism in the Soviet Union have strongly stimulated the working people and land-oppressed peoples of the world to rise up and struggle for self-liberation and to build a new life for themselves. The experiences of the great October Revolution and of socialist construction in the Soviet Union are of tremendous significance for the international Communist movement as a whole.

The great Communist Party of China has led the people's democratic revolution to victory and is taking the 650 million Chinese people to socialism. Following the victory of the Soviet October Revolution, the victory of the Chinese Revolution is of tremendous historic significance. The victory of the Chinese Revolution and the achievements recorded by China in the building of socialism have dealt crippling blows to imperialism and helped the balance of world forces tip in favor of the socialist camp and world peace. They are strongly stimulating the national liberation movement and the revolutionary struggle of the world's peoples.

The Soviet Union and China, and the Communist Party of the Soviet Union and the Communist Party of China, have very great strength and prestige. Close solidarity between the Soviet Union and China, between the Communist Party of the Soviet Union and the Communist Party of China, is of special importance. The Lao Dong Party always defends the Soviet Union, China, and the other fraternal countries in the socialist camp and unceasingly makes all-out efforts to contribute to strengthening the unity between the Soviet Union and China, the unity of the socialist camp, and the unity of the international Communist and workers' movement on the basis of Marxism-Leninism and the 1957 Moscow Declaration and the 1960 Moscow Statement.

Recently a number of brother parties proposed that the parties stop criticizing one another in the press and over the radio and make active preparations for the holding of a meeting of representatives of Communist and workers' parties. Proceeding from its sincere desire to strengthen unity within the international Communist movement, the Politburo of the Lao Dong Party Central Committee welcomes such views and deems it necessary to recall the proposal previously made by our party. We propose the following concrete points:

1. The Communist and workers' parties should stop all reciprocal criticisms in the press, over the radio, and so on,

and avoid any actions likely to bring about further mis-understanding and differences in order to create favorable conditions for the convening of a meeting of representatives of Communist and workers' parties.

2. That a meeting of Communist and workers' parties is aimed at further assessing together the situation and the tasks of the international Communist and workers' movement, and together discussing and settling divergences of views in order to strengthen unity and coordinate actions for common goals of struggle.

3. The Communist Party of the Soviet Union and the Communist Party of China have the greatest share of responsibility in preparing all necessary conditions for bringing that international meeting to achieve good results.

We think that in the present situation such an international meeting as was mentioned above needs careful preparations. We hold, however, that these preparations should be speedy so that the meeting can be held as early as possible. We earnestly call on all fraternal parties and all Communists to make active contributions to restore unity and to avoid all that may create further discords.

Sharing the view of many fraternal parties, we hold that within the international Communist movement at present discords are only temporary. We firmly believe that, with the common efforts of all Communist and workers' parties, we will overcome that situation and strengthen unity within the international Communist movement, and that under the surely victorious banner of Marxism-Leninism we will march shoulder to shoulder toward greater successes in the common struggle against imperialism and for peace, national independence, democracy, and socialism.

A COMPARISON
OF CERTAIN JOINT STATEMENTS

The manner and the extent of DRV concessions to the viewpoint of distinguished Communist visitors during their presence in North Vietnam are exemplified by the following comparisons made between the texts of two joint statements issued by Ho Chi Minh and a visitor. The first joint statement is that signed by President Ho Chi Minh and Antonín Novotný, President of Czechoslovakia, on January 26, 1963, referred to below as Statement A; the second is that signed by Ho Chi Minh and Chairman Liu Shao-chi of China on May 16, 1963, referred to as Statement B.

1. *AGREEMENT*

STATEMENT A:

"In an atmosphere full of friendship, the two sides are completely unanimous on all questions discussed. . . ."

STATEMENT B:

"The talks were held in an extremely sincere, cordial, and friendly atmosphere."

Comment: The difference in the wording suggests that Ho Chi Minh and Liu Shao-chi were unable to agree on all matters discussed, and this is borne out by the omission from their statement of references to peaceful coexistence and by the attribution of certain passages to either Ho Chi Minh or

Liu Shao-chi. All passages in Statement A are attributed to both signatories.

2. THE WORLD SITUATION

STATEMENT A:

"The representatives of the two countries have reviewed the world situation and note that the forces of peace, national independence, democracy, and socialism have developed and consolidated day by day. The socialist countries are taking vigorous steps in their economic construction and developing the great influence of the world socialist system on the evolution of the world situation. The Soviet Union, the center of the world socialist camp, is making great strides forward in building communism and is leading the world in advanced branches of science and technology. China and the other brother socialist countries are also recording big achievements in building socialism. The CPSU, the party of the great Lenin, the tested and experienced vanguard of the international Communist movement, and the Communist and workers' parties of other countries continue to exert their great influence upon the development of human society."

STATEMENT B:

"Both parties unanimously hold that the present international situation is favorable to the revolutionary struggle of the people of various countries but unfavorable to imperialism and the reactionaries of various countries. The might of the socialist camp has become more powerful. The national-democratic revolutionary movement in Asia, Africa, and Latin America is on a continual upsurge. The struggles of the working class and the masses of the people in the developed capitalist countries against monopoly capital, for improved living conditions, and for democratic rights have seen new development. The movement of the people of the world against the imperialist policies of aggression and war and in the defense of world peace is growing in breadth and depth. The general crisis of capitalism is daily deepening. The contradictions among the imperialist powers, especially between United States imperialism and other imperialist powers, have become more and more acute. The imperialist camp is heading further toward disintegration. The emergence of this situation is the result of the protracted struggle by the socialist camp and the people of the world against imperialism and the reactionaries, and the result of mutual support and joint struggle by the great forces of our time, namely the forces of the socialist camp, the forces of the national liberation movement, the forces of the international working class movement, and the forces of the peace movement, and particularly the forces of the socialist camp and those of the national liberation movement. But the aggressive nature of imperialism will never change. The more it approaches its doom, the more it will give frenzied and desperate kicks. United States imperialism is redoubling its efforts in pushing ahead with its aggressive war plans, actively fostering the reactionary forces of various countries, and particularly the militarist forces of West Germany and Japan, and is increasing its attacks on the peoples of the world. It is engaged in frenzied arms expansion and war preparations, getting ready to fight both a nuclear war and conventional wars, and is already waging 'special warfare.' "

Comment: Note the peaceful nature of Statement A on the international situation, consonant with a policy of peaceful coexistence, and the belligerent nature of Statement B, with its references to war, to struggle, and to national liberation movements. Statement B omits references to the CPSU and the Soviet Union.

3. DISARMAMENT

STATEMENT A:

"The two sides hold that the most urgent problem in the present world situation is to struggle continuously for settling the question of general and complete disarmament. They are of the opinion that the drafts advanced by the Soviet Union constitute a basis for settling this very important question. The two countries will continue striving to impel the imperialist circles, who have so far obstinately repudiated general and complete disarmament, to constructive and concrete negotiations. The two sides attach particular importance to the question of ending nuclear weapons tests. They hold that it is necessary to strive to reach an agreement providing for the definite cessation of nuclear tests. The representatives of the two countries declare that they are in favor of a rapid liquidation of military bases abroad and withdrawal of troops from other countries' territories. In connection with the problem of general and complete disarmament the governments of the DRV and the Socialist Republic of Czechoslovakia have on many occasions expressed the will to take part in the elaboration and realization of measures likely to relax world tension and help create a favorable atmosphere in relations among states, such as the formation of atom-free zones in Central Europe, the Far East, and other parts of the world, the conclusion of a nonaggression pact between the member states of NATO and those of the Warsaw Treaty Organization, and the prohibition of war propaganda."

STATEMENT B:

"The two parties hold that to preserve world peace, to stop imperialism from launching a new world war, and to prevent a nuclear war the peoples of the world must heighten their vigilance and further join hands to form the broadest possible united front and wage an indefatigable struggle against imperialism headed by the United States and its lackeys. The two parties firmly believe that in the present time, when the forces of socialism have surpassed those of imperialism, and the forces of peace have surpassed those of war, it is possible to safeguard peace, prevent a world war, and prevent a nuclear war by relying on the unity and struggle of the masses of the people of all countries and on the proletarian parties of various countries. The two parties stand for general disarmament, for the total prohibition of the use, stockpiling, manufacture, and testing of nuclear weapons in the Pacific region including the United States of America. The two parties believe that through persistent struggle by the people of various countries it is possible to force imperialism to accept certain agreements on disarmament and an agreement to ban nuclear weapons. In the circumstances in which imperialism rejects disarmament and continues preparations for a nuclear war, it is highly necessary to strengthen the national defense might of the countries in the socialist camp, including the development of nuclear superiority of the socialist countries. . . ."

Comment: Note the more belligerent tone of Statement B throughout and particularly the apparent approval given by the DRV to Chinese development of nuclear weapons. Again Statement B omits any reference to the Soviet Union.

4. *CUBA*

STATEMENT A:

"The two sides hold that, thanks to the resolute stand of the Cuban people and government, thanks to the persistent efforts and firm and correct measures of the Soviet Union, and at the same time to the support of the other socialist countries and all forces of peace in the world, it was possible recently to stay the invasion of Cuba by United States imperialist forces, to safeguard the fruits of the Cuban revolution, and to discard the imminent danger of a devastating nuclear war. The two sides express their admiration for the valiant struggle of the Cuban people to defend the fatherland and declare total support for the five demands of the Cuban Government."

STATEMENT B:

"The two parties express immense admiration for the heroic Cuban people, who have won great victories in their struggle against United States imperialist aggression and in defense of their sovereignty, dignity, and fruits of revolution. Both parties are unanimous in their support for the five just demands put forward by Fidel Castro, leader of the Cuban people's revolution. The two parties note with satisfaction that the revolutionary ideas of the "Havana Declarations" are exerting an ever greater influence among the Latin American countries where the national-democratic movement is surging daily."

Comment: Note the complete omission from Statement B of any mention of Soviet actions in Cuba and the emphasis placed upon revolution in Latin America.

5. INDIA

STATEMENT A:

"The two sides express their satisfaction at the decision of November 21, 1962 of the Chinese Government on cease-fire and withdrawal of troops in the Sino-Indian border areas and its readiness to negotiate with the Indian side. At the same time they welcome the efforts made by the six countries meeting recently in Colombo and by other Asian and African countries to speed up the peaceful settlement of the Sino-Indian boundary problem. They express the hope that China and India, the two great countries of Asia, will find a just and honorable solution to the border problem in conformity with the interests of both peoples and to the benefit of the consolidation of Asian-African solidarity and the maintenance of peace in Asia and the world."

STATEMENT B:

"The Government of the DRV firmly supports the consistent stand of the Government of the CPR for a peaceful settlement of the Sino-Indian boundary question through negotiations. It warmly praises the cease-fire, the withdrawal of the Chinese frontier guards, the release of all captured Indian military personnel, and other important measures taken by China on its own initiative, and deems that these measures fully demonstrate China's sincere desire to seek a peaceful settlement of the Sino-Indian boundary question. President Ho Chi Minh expresses the hope that China and India may quickly start direct negotiations for a peaceful settlement of the Sino-Indian boundary question."

Comment: Note that Statement B omits all mention of the six Colombo countries and, indeed, seeks to exclude them from further negotiations by the use of the word "direct" in the reference to future negotiations. It makes no reference to India's being a great Asian country.

6. *PEACEFUL COEXISTENCE*

STATEMENT A:

"Its successes in construction and its policy of peaceful coexistence and friendly cooperation among nations have heightened the prestige of the Socialist Republic of Czechoslovakia in the world and have helped consolidate the solidarity, increase the strength, and broaden the international influence of the socialist camp as a whole."

Statement B ignores the policy of peaceful coexistence.

7. *REVISIONISM*

Statement A says nothing about revisionism or modern revisionism.

STATEMENT B:

"Both parties uphold the correct thesis in the 1957 Declaration and the 1960 Statement that in the present circumstances revisionism — in other words right opportunism — is the main danger in the international Communist movement. Revisionism, or right opportunism, is a manifestation of bourgeois ideology. It seeks persistently to kill the revolutionary spirit of Marxism-Leninism, deny the historical need of proletarian revolution and the dictatorship of the proletariat in the period of transition from capitalism to socialism and communism, paralyze the revolutionary will of the working class and laboring people, and undermine their confidence in socialism."

8. YUGOSLAVIA

Statement A does not mention Yugoslavia.

STATEMENT B:

"Yugoslav revisionism is the concentrated expression of modern revisionist 'theories.' The Yugoslav revisionist clique has betrayed Marxism-Leninism, has led Yugoslavia out of the socialist camp, and is engaged in sabotage against the socialist camp and the world Communist movement, and in activities detrimental to the unity of all peace-loving forces and countries. Further exposure of the Yugoslav revisionist clique remains an essential task of the Marxist-Leninist parties of all countries."

9. PEACEFUL EVOLUTION

Statement A makes no mention of peaceful evolution.

STATEMENT B:

"In regard to the socialist countries, United States imperialism, besides perpetrating military aggression and war threats, is intensifying subversion and infiltration and is pushing ahead with its policy of peaceful evolution, vainly attempting to have capitalism restored in these countries."

EPILOGUE

During the weeks that have elapsed since the writing of this book the quarrel between the Soviet Union and Communist China has developed with ever increasing momentum. Mutual recriminations have grown more and more bitter, and moderation has been rejected. The high point of the dispute during this period has been the conclusion of the partial nuclear test ban treaty. China not only has refused to sign that document but has also made it the basis of some of her most unrestrained attacks against the Soviet Union.

The situation of the DRV has grown extremely precarious, for, although no formal break has yet come about between China and the Soviet Union, Ho Chi Minh has been faced with the necessity of making a choice between the two which even he, consummate politician though he is, could not escape. Since all states were invited to sign the partial nuclear test ban treaty, the DRV was obliged to state publicly whether she would or would not sign. No evasion was possible, nor was there any room for doubt that, in the case of Communist states, to sign was to align oneself with the Soviet Union and to refuse was to take the side of China. North Vietnam has now publicly refused to sign.

By this action she has bowed to the inevitable and aligned herself with China. Doubtless if the opportunity were to arise, the DRV would once again seek to regain her earlier position of neutrality, but the possibilities for so doing appear daily more remote as a formal break between the Communist giants becomes imminent. Moreover, by her refusal to sign the treaty the DRV has committed so grievous an affront to the Soviet Union that it is questionable whether she can ever again restore her former relationship with that country.

Having made his fateful decision, Ho Chi Minh appears to be seeking closer links with China, and DRV statements on all topics have increasingly tended to reflect Chinese rather than Soviet views. Independent evidence also points to the deterioration of relations between the Soviet Union and North Vietnam. To cite one of many examples, neutralist Laotian General Kong Le on his return from Moscow in early October asked the Thai government to grant permission for Soviet military aid to his troops to be routed across Thailand. He stated by way of explanation that it was no longer possible for the Soviet Union to send such supplies through China and North Vietnam.

Under these circumstances it is well within the bounds of possibility that the Soviet Union will decide to withdraw her own and East European technicians from North Vietnam, leaving DRV industrial development at a standstill. Should the Soviets do so, the plight of North Vietnam would become grave.

For several reasons, climatic as well as political, the tenth-month rice harvest of 1963 in North Vietnam has been disastrously bad, a large part of the crop being lost. This has faced the DRV with her greatest food shortage to date. For the first time the North Vietnamese government has sought to purchase supplies of Australian wheat through the Hong Kong firm of Jardine Matheson, which handles similar transactions for the Chinese government. The Vietnamese attempt was unsuccessful, however, because she was unable to offer any satisfactory form of payment.

During the months of August and September 1963 Ho Chi Minh approached President Ngo Dinh Diem of South Vietnam with requests that the latter should demand the departure of United States military personnel and should declare South Vietnam a neutral state. In return Ho was prepared to offer very generous terms, including the cessation of Vietcong attacks. His principal reason for adopting such a course was to obtain access to South Vietnamese rice, but it is highly unlikely that his overtures will meet with any success.

Thus, in a matter of only a few weeks, the situation of the DRV, both economic and international, has deteriorated to a very marked degree. There is still no sign that President Ho Chi Minh has found any way out from a position that can justly be described as desperate.

P. J. H.

October 8, 1963

INDEX

Date Due